THE RETURN

The Return

28 things to look for before Jesus comes

BILL McKEE

Tyndale House
Publishers, Inc.
Wheaton, Illinois

Library of Congress Catalog Card Number 79-63784
ISBN 0-8423-7021-8
Copyright © 1972 by Tyndale House Publishers,
Wheaton, Illinois. All rights reserved.
Second printing, October 1979
Printed in the United States of America

Previously published under the title *Orbit of Ashes*.

This book is lovingly dedicated to

my wife Sharon,

whose encouragement and confidence

helped make it possible

CONTENTS

Chapter 2   /   Up, Up and Away   69

First the Dead
Then Us
Face to Face
Who's Going to Be Here?
What Now?
The Fire Falls
Order Your Crown Now
The Marriage Banquet

Chapter 3   /   2,555 Days of Bad News   81

Wrath
Wrath Plus Mercy Equals Hope
144,000 Jews Get It On
The Dynamic Duo
War in Heaven
The Devil's Disciple
The Enforcer
666

Chapter 4   /   The Wrath of God   97

The Seals

The Trumpets
The Bowls (Vials)

Chapter 5/Death of the Spiritual Whore   101

Babylon's Last Ride

Chapter 6   /   Armageddon   107

Kingdoms in Conflict
Russia Pulls the Trigger
Forward, March—to Death
Meanwhile, Back with the Beast
A Ghastly Replay
Challenge from the East
Diabolical Double-Cross
Leap Frog
Look Up—and Die!
The Mountain Splits
Lake of Fire
The Super Supper

Chapter 7   /   Peace at Last   127

The Kingdom Come
How Sweet It Is
We Will Rule
Look Out! Satan's Loose
The Great White Throne
The Book
The World's on Fire
The Lord's City
Majesty! Glory! Power!

INTRODUCTION

If you drive carefully and take care of yourselves, you may be around to see the most phenomenal event in world history—*the return of Jesus Christ to earth.*

When he was here before, he told his disciples what to expect: they wouldn't know the day or hour of his return, but the clues he'd give would help identify the general time. His disciples passed these clues, or signs, on to the following generations—and I'm convinced we are the generation to see his return! But we must be on the lookout, or we will be caught unawares—just like the many skeptics who have no clue to his coming.

The Second Coming is referred to 380 times in the New Testament alone. Only four books of the twenty-seven omit a reference to it, so it doesn't take a superintellect to reason that God is trying to get our attention about something important. God doesn't want you to be uninformed about his Son's coming. In 1 Thessalonians 4:16-18 he had Paul clearly tell us how Christians will rocket away to meet him in the clouds:

"For the Lord himself will come down from heaven with a mighty shout and with the soul-stirring cry of the archangel and the great trumpet call of God. And the believers who are dead will be the first to rise to meet the Lord. Then we who are still alive and remain on the earth will be caught up with them in the clouds to meet the Lord in the air and remain with him forever. So comfort and encourage each other with this news" *(TLB).

---

*Most of the scripture references quoted in this book are from *The Living Bible*, © 1971 Tyndale House Publishers.

ALL-POINTS ALERT!

Alert 1

No Way—They Say!

"First, I want to remind you that in the last days there will come scoffers who will do every wrong they can think of, and laugh at the truth. This will be their line of argument: So Jesus promised to come back, did he? Then where is he? He'll never come!

"He isn't really being slow about his promised return, even though it sometimes seems that way. But he is waiting, for the good reason that he is not willing that any should perish, and he is

giving more time for sinners to repent. The day
of the Lord is surely coming, as unexpectedly as
a thief" (2 Peter 3:3, 4a, 9, 10a).

How come, then, that so many pastors and
theologians either deny it altogether or express
doubt about it?

Well, those who know see these scoffers as another sign of Jesus' coming. We don't expect
unbelievers to see this sign, but it's Alert Number
One for Christians!

Alert 2

Stains on the Steeple

When you see the church become like the world, coddling it instead of warning it about sin and judgment, look out—and up!

Paul writes: "But the Holy Spirit tells us clearly that in the last times some in the church will turn away from Christ and become eager followers of teachers with devil-inspired ideas. These teachers will tell lies with straight faces and do it so often that their consciences won't even bother them" (1 Timothy 4:1, 2).

Many Christian seminaries today turn out "ministers" who will never lead a person to faith in Jesus. Their teachers have taught them to be "intellectually honest" and "socially concerned," but haven't shown them the necessity of faith or trained them in God's Word.

"For there is going to come a time when people won't listen to the truth, but will go around looking for teachers who will tell them just what they want to hear. They won't listen to what the Bible says, but will blithely follow their own misguided ideas" (2 Timothy 4:3, 4).

That time has come! A well-known slogan may well typify this generation: Don't confuse me with the facts; my mind is made up!"

Some churches are preaching ecology, social reform, civil rights, and world peace. These are critical issues for everyone—but they are not the gospel committed to the Church. The Church can't major in minors—and still make beautiful music for God. Pretty subtle: stay busy doing good so there's no time to do the best. . . .

Don't you be faked out. It's a sign of the end.

Alert 3

Blow in My Ear . . . I'll Follow You Anywhere

Just think of the millions of people who try to follow the stars they can't see by means of astrological charts they can't read—made up by astrologers who can't resist the gullibility of people! Why, almost anybody could write those verbal tranquilizers that are gulped down by the gullible everywhere. For example:

Hi, star-starers and planet-peekers! This is your orbit ogler, charting the course for today's dazzling destiny.

Aries—Don't be mad at someone you like. Try to do the best you can at what you're best at trying.

Taurus—Since your sign is the bull, stay out of Mexico.

Gemini-Crickets—Insects have an adverse effect on your concentration, so don't be upset when things bug you.

Cancer—It's no laughing matter.

Leo—Please don't be catty, even if your friends
    are lion.

Virgo—Smile a little more; the cast should be
    off by Wednesday.

Libra—Consult with kin about whether you can.
    If you find you can't cut it with your kin,
    can the whole thing and consult me
    tomorrow.

Scorpio—Stop hiding under rocks and remem-
    ber you are the greatest with detail.

Sagittarius—Enjoy the food you like. But re-
    member you have a tendency to Sag-
    ittarius, and that's heavy.

Capricorn—Invest in stalks, preferably corn.
    Keep your ears open for opportunities
    in the military. You are colonel material.
    Don't cob out!

Aquarius—Variable cloudiness with a 99 per-
    cent chance of failure. Now have a nice
    day.

Pisces—Your star has been misplaced, but hang
    in there. A misplaced star usually means
    you'll die, but this is not your lucky
    day. I'm almost certain I can find an-
    other star for you by tomorrow . . . if
    you make it.

Today there is fantastic interest in reincarna-
tion, gurus, devil worship, seances, fortune-tellers,
the occult, and supernatural phenomena. Ever
wonder why?

In 2 Timothy 4, the Bible tells us people will
"turn aside to many myths." In chapter 3, we

read that "in the last days, people will be forever following new teachers, but they'll never understand the truth." We need to understand that God hates astrology; that's right, he *hates* it! He knows it isn't a harmless little game or a cute collection of birthday predictions—it's a *religion,* a form of worship that he zapped as far back as Genesis. I've read that the tower of Babel (Genesis 2) was actually a gigantic ziggurat, or observatory tower, for astrologers. As you know, God "finished" the project before they got it working.

This was Babylon, the empire known for wickedness and total disdain for God and his prophets. Throughout history Babylon-types have invented new ways to reject God and worship idols. But these early Chaldeans (the intellects) were clever enough to devise a way to con not only the common people but kings and philosophers as well.

They divided the skies into twelve parts—the zodiac, we call it—and said the stars and planets control human life. They were the only ones who could accurately read the stars, of course, so they became the priests over man's destiny. This was so destructive a sin that we find astrologers condemned to death in Deuteronomy 18. Isaiah 47 predicts God's devastation of Babylon worshipers and Chaldean astrologers.

This demonic religion is back in style—a sign from God that spiritual pollution needs a global cleanup by the Purifier from heaven.

The Good, the Bad, and the Ugly

Jesus said, "The gospel of the kingdom will be preached throughout the whole world, as a testimony to all nations, and then the end will come" (Matthew 24:14).

As a foreign missionary, I have had a part in seeing this good prophecy being fulfilled. I don't know of a single nation that has not heard the gospel. Many, like South Korea and some African countries, are more Christian than the U. S. By means of radio and literature, the message is spreading fast and far. I've been in villages where the language has never been written, but where there is a church and a strong group of believers. Pretuned radios bring the gospel in their dialect every day. So this good sign is happening now.

An interesting development among churches is the tendency to merge. Already some denominations have merged and there are plans for others to "get together." Nine of the larger Protestant denominations are members of the Consultation on Church Union (COCU) which aims to join 20 million U. S. church-goers in the '70s.

This ecumenical movement isn't new. Some leaders have been trying for years to unite the Roman Catholic, Greek Orthodox, and Protestant churches into one world church. The final result of this effort is described in Revelation 17. "Babylon the Great" is a combination of apostasy, priestcraft, and atheism.

The apostates once knew the truth, but they no longer preach Christ, his Word, and his resurrection; their churches are social clubs with easy membership and unnoticed departures. Priests have misdirected faith away from the invisible God to the ornate system and taught people that their good works will qualify them for heaven, in spite of what God says in Ephesians 2:8, 9.

And did you ever imagine you'd hear of "Christian atheists"? That's a sign of our times too. Some ministers hopped on the "God-is-dead" wagon without the slightest urging. God calls them "clouds without rain," empty balloons blown about by gusty trends. Paul wrote about them in 2 Timothy 3:5—"Having a form of godliness, but denying the power thereof: from such, turn away."

Then there's the ugly—the opposite of the true Church who have been born into God's family through personal faith in Jesus Christ as Savior and Lord and are also called Jesus' "bride." Believers are beautiful and are loved by Jesus even though we are far from perfect. But the "church" that respects Christ without worshiping him and repeats his words without obeying them is a spiritual monster, not his bride!

Everyone is religious. Pagan tribes worship rocks, trees, the sun—something! Having lived in the Orient, I've seen the idols, the temples, the fear, and even the bloodshed (by the flagellantes in the Philippines) that make up religion. But the gods never answer. The eyes of an old Buddhist returning from his friend's funeral signal that there is no hope, nothing but dread. Some speak of Nirvana, meditation, flower gardens, and Yoga. It sounds neat—until you have to die.

The One I trust defeated death—and said I would, too! That, friend, is living hope!

The division between the false and true followers of Christ is very evident right now. The counterfeit bride will be left waiting at the altar—in the devil's "church"—and in the darkness mistake the Antichrist for the Bridegroom! (Matthew 24:4, 5)

Alert 7

What If Nobody Gave a War and Everybody Came?

If I tried to make a big deal out of another war in our sick world, you'd probably say, "What else is new!" In fact, any of these "alerts" isn't very impressive alone. It's when you put all of these happenings together in one generation that it becomes *very* impressive, and only a blind man would deny it.

Jesus said in Matthew 24:6, 7, "You will be hearing about wars and rumors of wars; see that you be not troubled; for they have to come." The rumor or threat of a nuclear war has caused more tension and anxiety than any war we've had. This problem is unique to our generation. God doesn't want us to miss the order.

He has limited himself—always for loves sake— numerous times. To Israel, to Nineveh, to all mankind when Christ died, and in entrusting humans with the life-saving gospel, God demonstrated his patience and mercy. Giving us the privilege of winning men and women to Christ instead of delegating it to angels was one of his greatest acts of love. That opportunity continues even in the midst of warfare.

"For nation shall rise against nation and kingdom against kingdom. . . ." Did you know that there have been forty-four wars since World War II? And though Vietnam was not a declared war, all the major nations took a position for or against the combatants there.

Another "aligning" factor involves Israel. Interestingly enough, nations against communism generally stand with Israel against the Arab nations. "And nation shall rise against nation and kingdom against kingdom. . . ."

Dag Hammarskjöld, the late Secretary General of the United Nations and Nobel Peace Prize winner, said, "I see no hope for a permanent world peace. We tried so hard and failed so miserably. Unless the world experiences a spiritual rebirth within the next few years, we are doomed."

A Loaf of Bread Will Buy a Bag of Gold

". . . and there will be famines . . ." (Matthew 24:7).

Yes, it's true that the world has always had some famine. Hunger and deprivation have become so common that we almost take it for granted. But I was moved when I *saw* starving people in Hong Kong, lying on the sidewalks and crammed into shacks, boats, or resettlement areas. Bodies were fished out of the harbors and taken off the streets before the tourists finished breakfast, but that didn't decrease the number. And reports of many suicides were hushed up and went unpublished.

With the world population exploding, especially in countries that can't feed the people they already have, the situation verges on crisis.

Jesus told us to watch for such signs. In Matthew 24:8 he compares these to birth pains. Nobody knows the moment of birth, but when the pains start it's time to take action. Drop everything; it's time to move!

Who could understand or forgive a mother who lost her baby because she didn't believe the "signs" of its coming? The signs of Jesus' coming are painful, too. Most of them are morally, economically, and sociologically distressing.

Jesus is telling us that the "nine months" are over: these are signs of birth! The wars, famines, earthquakes, and other alerts are intensifying and becoming more frequent. God is trying to get our attention. Let's not blow it by thinking we have lots of time.

A *New York Times* report reminds us of Christ's warning signs. Here is an excerpt:

"Imagine the entire population of Missouri and Kentucky, seven million people, fleeing their states and taking refuge in central and southern Illinois. That thought gives some idea of the dimensions of what is happening now in East Pakistan—except that the refugees are much poorer and the area into which they are fleeing infinitely more desperate than Illinois.

British sources estimate that between four and five million East Pakistanis have crossed into India, and that 100,000 more are leaving every day. Before long, the total could be seven or eight million.

The refugees are in a country that already has difficulty feeding itself, one afflicted by overpopulation and unemployment. There are no jobs for the refugees, and no farmland. They are starting to filter into Calcutta, a city where one million people regularly sleep on the pavement and millions more have no water or sewage systems.

The India-Pakistan War killed many thousands of civilians. No one will ever know exactly how many, but some observers have put the figure as high as several hundred thousand.

The human and economic dislocation now threatens to lead to a terrible famine. The *Financial Times* of London, which is not given to exaggeration, has published an estimate that up to four million people in East Pakistan may die in the coming month. . . ."

Shake, Rattle, and Roll

Can you see one of the "Jesus People" approach a guy in Pasadena, California, the day before the earthquakes, and say, "S'cuse me, Clyde, but did you know that Jesus said, 'In the last days there will be earthquakes, famine, and . . .'?"

"Get outta here, weirdo," answers Clyde. "Who believes that stuff? Go get a haircut and take a load off your mind." Guess who becomes a believer the following morning when he's blown out of bed by one of *many* quakes.

I can see Clyde under his sink yelling, "Where's that beautiful long-haired Jesus guy! I believe! I believe!"

Matthew 24:7 notes: ". . . and earthquakes in many places . . ." Scientists are so concerned about the increase of earthquakes all over the world that they are spending millions studying the problem. If you read newspapers or watch television, you know about the extensive death and destruction caused by earthquakes within a short time. I watched a panel of experts tell the people of California that the quakes and tremors (over 200 of them) were not where they were expected to be, nor were they as severe as later earthquakes will be.

Later I saw a film of people building houses right where other houses were destroyed. Whew! To lose a house because you ignore signs is sad, but to lose your soul by rejecting warnings is tragic.

In Luke 21, plagues are also mentioned as a sign of the coming of Jesus for his people. Outbreaks of cholera, flu, and other diseases are increasing in India, Pakistan, and other countries. If we continue to pollute our water and air, we may see rampant disease in many countries.

Alert 10

How Far, Superstar?

"Then there will be strange events in the skies—
warnings, evil omens, and portents in sun, moon,
and stars; and down here on earth the nations
will be in turmoil, perplexed by the roaring seas
and strange tides. The courage of many people
will falter because of the fearful fate they see coming upon the earth, for the stability of the very
heavens will be broken up. Then the peoples of
the earth shall see me, *the man from heaven,* coming in a cloud with power and great glory, so when
all these things begin to happen, stand straight
and look up! For your salvation is near" (Luke
21:25-28).

The final fulfillment of what you have just read
will take place in the last days of the Great Tribulation. But the beginnings of such things are happening *now*.

Regardless of how old you are, you probably
didn't expect men actually to walk on the moon.
Nor did we imagine watching and listening to them

as well!

What stranger things could there be than UFOs? We used to laugh and put them down. We're not too amused anymore. Sightings by pilots and other reliable people cause us to suspend our judgment.

If Russia or the U. S. explodes a powerful missile on the moon, what might happen to the ocean tides on earth which are controlled by the moon?

It's startling to realize that the communication system for the future world dictator may be in orbit right now. We have all watched events on the other side of the world as they happen, via Telstar. Just the thing for communication between Big Brother and his slaves!

Some people point to our freaky weather as an indication that the "stability of the heavens" is already broken. It seems as if we've had more tornadoes, hurricanes, typhoons, tidal waves, and so forth, but only the people who are looking up will see and recognize the signs. Other people will have their heads in the sands of money-making, pleasure, politics, and social reform through science and psychology. What an awful blast all that will be!

Alert 11

The Last Thump of the Pump

"Men's hearts shall fail them for fear" (Luke 21:26).

The number-one killer in the United States is heart failure and heart disease. It wasn't always this way. Doctors can tell you that this problem was almost rare in past generations, so the very center of life within man is warning him of Christ's coming. If man doesn't get any message from the heavens, the earthquakes, the famine and disease; if he doesn't react against the bizarre cults, the phonies, the scoffers, or pseudo churches, he can hear the message in his chest.

Jesus said: "In the same way, when you see the events taking place that I've described, you can be just as sure that the kingdom of God is near. I solemnly declare to you that when these things happen, the end of this age has come. Watch out! Don't let me find you living in careless ease, carousing and drinking, and occupied with the problems of this life, like the rest of the

world. Don't let my sudden coming catch you unawares. Keep a constant watch. And pray that
if possible, you may arrive in my presence without
having to experience these horrors" (Luke 2:31,
33, 36).

Why Do You Think They Call It Dope?

In Revelation 9:21; 21:8; and 22:15, the words "sorcerer" and "sorceries" appear. This is *pharmakeia* in Greek, from which we got "pharmacy." A literal translation defines the word as "the practice of drugging or poisoning." Early use of drugs was usually associated with occult or black magic activities.

Unless you've been in a coma the last few years, you are aware that many in the U. S. are in "the practice of drugging or poisoning" themselves. Users and scholars alike rationalize this as a mere trend or fad of the times. Some far-out types insist drugs are mind-liberating medicines. This is another example of man's irrationalism unaided by the wisdom of the Holy Spirit. We understand, then, how "they shall be made to believe a lie" (2 Thessalonians 2:11). The very opposite of the truth is readily accepted by those who have flatly rejected *the* Truth. This problem is mentioned in the last book of the Bible because the sign and the book alert us to the events and trends of Jesus' coming.

Alert 13

The Devil Made Me Do It

Evil activities in the world today carry a hint of panic—as if the perpetrators are anxious about the time left for their machinations. Satan doesn't know exactly when Jesus will come for his people, but Satan can see the same signs we do—and he *believes* them.

We should know more about our archenemy . . .

1. He's the god of this world. Satan and his evil ways are followed by those who have rejected the true God, and Satan has "rewarded" his people with spiritual blindness (2 Corinthians 4:4). Christians were once in the same doomed crowd, as Paul describes in Ephesians 2:1, 2—"Once you were under God's curse, doomed forever for your sins. You went along with the crowd and were just like all the others, full of sin, obeying Satan, the mighty prince of the power of the air, who is at work right now in the hearts of those who are against the Lord."

2. He's a master of disguises. In 2 Corinthians

11:13-15 Paul warns Christians about ministers who are phony leaders. He says, "Satan can change himself into an angel of light . . . and seem like godly ministers"—or shall we say, like groovy guys.

He's a smooth, good-looking dude who says sex is good anytime with anyone; purity is passé; immorality is moral now; and love is lust. He's got millions of admirers who think pleasure is free because the payments don't come due till death . . . and hell.

He's a bearded gentleman with a soothing tongue and quiet charm. He politely mocks Christian faith and makes it seem anti-intellectual. His manner is pleasing, and since the wrong is popular it's tough to stand for the right. A "new position" seems in order—and the devil chuckles as the Christian advances to the rear.

As a swinging free spirit he fakes restless young people into a dead-end detour just across the bridge from the highway of faith.

Satan is these and more. Sometimes he sets aside the disguises and comes on as the beast he really is. "Be careful—watch out for attacks from Satan, your great enemy. He prowls around like a hungry, roaring lion, looking for some victim to tear apart" (1 Peter 5:8).

There are "satanic churches" in America's major cities today. Record albums have been dedicated to him. Movies present him as a clever intriguing spirit. Book stores offer indoctrination in the ways of black magic, warlocks, witchcraft, occult practices, and Satan worship.

He's out to get us in these last days. By cleverly
diverting attention to "ripping off the establishment," marching, boycotting, renewing, or whatever, he keeps people from noticing that Jesus is
coming.

Trouble is ahead even for "Big Five Christians"
—(attenders of Sunday school, morning worship,
young people's, evening service, and prayer meet-
ing). Pride is the pitfall. God doesn't need observers; he needs workers. He calls us to holy
living, not holy appearances. We must be involved
in loving and sharing burdens and winning people
to Jesus to prevent ingrown eyeballs, the affliction
generated by spiritual nitpicking and assessment of
others' defects.

The devil has used the negative, loveless Christians and apostate churchmen who deny Christ's
deity to turn off a generation of young people.
One told me, "I dig Jesus, man; I just can't stand
his disciples."

Thank God for the Jesus Revolution; God said
when evil abounds, his grace would abound even
more.

Remember: "God is light and in him is no
darkness at all" (1 John 1:5). He has revealed
himself three ways: as a human being; through
his Word; and by his Spirit in the believer. We
can know God intimately and increasingly, if we
sincerely desire to.

But Satan asks to be trusted in the dark. Things
like Ouija boards, astrology, fortune-telling, sean-

ces, and drugs that ask your faith—even a silly millimeter of it—without identifying the source of information is suspect, maybe satanic. He needs only a crack in the door to sneak into the heart. Without Jesus, the disease is fatal!

What a Blast!

Scientists proudly accept credit for splitting the atom and developing the hydrogen bomb—while no small army marches regularly to psychiatric consultations for fear of nuclear extinction. Nations talk disarmament but stockpile weapons that are increasingly effective for wiping out whole populations. Ironically, man is beginning to produce the kind of power that God may use to end human history and start a new, clean chapter.

In 2 Peter 3 and Isaiah 34 the Bible speaks of such intense heat that elements will melt and the earth will dissolve. I imagine that the intellectuals in Isaiah's day laughed and mocked when he predicted that. They were probably marveling that a sword can have two sharp edges and exclaiming: "What will man think of next!"

Do you remember Hiroshima? There the atom bomb was first dropped on people. Some of the grotesque results were hard to believe. Listen to this: "Their flesh shall waste away while they are standing on their feet; their eyes shall corrode in their sockets, and their tongues shall decay in their mouths." Does that sound like Hiroshima? It's from Zechariah 14:12, and the site is noted: "This shall be the plague with which the Lord shall smite all the people who have waged war against Jerusalem."

This event will take place after Jesus has taken his people to heaven, but the heat-blast can already be felt by atom-watchers. How tragic that man can dig his own grave and call it building world peace!

Where Are You Going So Slowly?

Man's technology and achievements are indeed impressive. Computers, organ transplants, and moon walks indicate remarkable intelligence and resourcefulness. However, crime, divorce, drug abuse, alcoholism, etc. increase. Man's wisdom and judgment are great, but they can't be fully trusted. He is concentrating on the wrong subjects and "breaking through" in the wrong direction.

I've been told that the high school diploma of today is equivalent to the college diploma of forty years ago—and I believe it. At universities most freshman textbooks become obsolete, revised, or replaced by graduation time four years later. But human-oriented knowledge won't do the job!

"So what about these wise men, these scholars, these brilliant debaters of this world's great affairs? God has made them all look foolish, and shown their wisdom to be useless nonsense" (1 Corinthians 1:20).

Is this a sign? An angel counseled: "But Daniel,

keep this prophecy a secret; seal it up so that it will not be understood until the end times when travel and education shall be vastly increased" (Daniel 12:4).

We can travel anywhere in the world now in a matter of hours. Travel agencies, friendly skies, special deals, go-now-pay-never. We've got lots of evidence that these indeed are the "last days."

"But the man who isn't a Christian can't accept these thoughts from God, which the Holy Spirit teaches us. They sound foolish to him. . . . But the spiritual man has insight into everything, and that bothers and baffles the man of the world, who can't understand him at all" (1 Corinthians 2:14, 15).

"So stop fooling yourself. If you count yourself above average in intelligence, as judged by this world's standards, you had better put this all aside (world's wisdom) and be a fool rather than let it hold you back from the true wisdom from above" (1 Corinthians 3:18).

Alert 17

Mafia on Welfare?

If crime doesn't pay, how come the Mafia isn't on welfare? OK! So crime *does* pay. People get away with murder—thanks to lawyers who love money and judges who strain at legal technicalities and swallow monstrous crimes.

The men who wrote the Constitution obviously knew human nature better than their descendants. Man's inborn nature is evil:

"For we naturally love to do evil things—when you follow your own wrong inclinations your lives will produce these results: impure thoughts, eagerness for lustful pleasure, idolatry, spiritism, hatred, fighting, jealousy, anger, constant effort to get the best for yourself, complaints, criticism, the feeling that everyone is wrong except those in your own little group, wrong doctrine, envy, murder, drunkenness, wild parties, and all that sort of thing. . . . Let me tell you again, as I have before, that anyone living that kind of life will not inherit the kingdom of God" (Galatians 5:17a, 18-21).

When laws are stretched to give freedom to guys like that, they'll trample people and run themselves into the ground. Thousands of students have been used by the mob manipulators. Using violence to stop violence proves you believe in violence. "Love and peace!" in one breath, and "Kill the pigs!" in the next indicate a sad logic.

There's a double standard in the new liberated law—the same double standard that always surrounds dishonest people, and it seems to be taking over society. There are judges who slap the wrists of pornographers, prostitutes, and pushers while laying the law on poor tenants who can't pay their rent. There are schools that ban prayer and hire Communists. There are people who grin at the chaos around them and sing, "Everything is beautiful!" It would be hilarious if it weren't so horrible.

God mercifully keeps warning man, but man staggers blindly on. Jesus told us society would disintegrate morally and be again like Sodom when he rained fire and brimstone on it, and like the whole world when he sent the flood in Noah's time. "And God saw that the wickedness of man was great in the earth, and that every imagination of the thoughts of his heart was only evil continually." "Even thus shall it be in the days when the Son of man is revealed" (Genesis 6:5; Luke 17:30).

Perverted sex—such as homosexuality and lesbianism—is evil to God no matter how "normal" the pollsters and social engineers make it. This is one of the reasons for God's anger and judgment against Sodom and Gomorrah. The word "sodomy," an unnatural sexual act, comes from the city Sodom! "Those who live immoral lives—who are idol worshipers, adulterers, or homosexuals—will have no share in his kingdom" (1 Corinthians 6:9, 10).

So lawlessness, violence, and sexual perversion abound in our world. Where can we look for help? Only those with the wisdom and insight given by the Holy Spirit will think to look up—and be delivered.

Ping-Pong Diplomacy Blows Up

China is definitely involved in the prophecy of the "last days." As backward and primitive as she may seem, and though Western economists laughed about her "Great Leap—Backwards!" of a few years ago, she is no longer a sleeping dragon, but a stalking dragon!

Revelation 16:12 refers to the "kings of the East." An army of 200 million is mentioned in Revelation 9:16. If you have ever doubted the absolute accuracy of the Bible and the integrity of those God inspired to write it, think about John when he was told to write down that figure. Can't you imagine John saying, "Excuse me, but you did mean 200 *thousand,* didn't you?" But John wrote it down, and it has been scoffed at for years—but not any more. An Associated Press release informed us of China's boasted "200 million armed and organized militiamen." Her role during the Tribulation will be to destroy one-third of all mankind!

How? In verse 18 it says by "smoke, fire, and flaming sulphur." If that verse had been written recently, it might have read something like this:

"Thousands of Chinese troops are massing on the banks of the Euphrates River. Their weaponry is more advanced and sophisticated than anyone could have guessed. They appear to have portable launching pads for huge space buses. These are loaded with dozens of high-megaton missiles that can be released from earth orbit by radio signals. The U. S., Canada, and South America have been warned not to interfere or they will be destroyed."

China developed a hydrogen bomb faster than any other country in the world. She is fully capable of performing her hideous destiny. I am convinced her friendly new stance will lead to further nuclear success.

A missionary from India told me he has been on a highway being built from China to the Mideast. Then a friend gave me an article by a special correspondent of the *Sunday Post,* published in Glasgow, Scotland (May 16, 1971). It reads:

SINISTER RACE ACROSS ROOF OF THE WORLD

A sinister race is being run by the two Communist superpowers, Russia and China. The course is over the mighty mountains that tower along their southern borders—the roof of the world. The prize is a tighter grip on the area. Ten years ago Russia started to build a 465-mile superhighway from the most southern inhabited point in the Russian state of Turkmenia. They finished it five years ago. Since then, they have been building feeder roads in Russia and Afghanistan. They now have a fast and direct overland route from their homeland to the Indian Ocean.

Not long ago the Chinese decided to build a similar all-weather four-lane highway through the mountains. It begins in Sinkiang, most southwesterly of all Chinese provinces. The road was finished two years ago and reduces a journey of two weeks to one of nine hours. They immediately began building a second road, this time in great secrecy. Twelve thousand Chinese were working on it and finished a few weeks ago. These roads conquer the formerly impassable Himalayas.

Why are these superpowers spending so much time, money, and effort on roads? Look at the map. The new highways are the thick black lines. Through these arteries they'll be able to pump raw materials, manufactured exports (and armies) to Arabia and the Middle East.

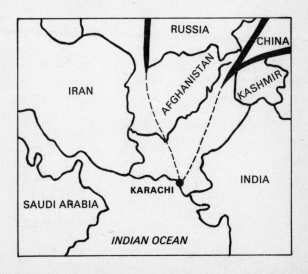

On the map you can see that India may be out-flanked by the Chinese.

The Russian Bear and Chinese Dragon are reaching out—to keep their prophetic appointment? In God's time!

The Big Red Machine Conks Out

Russia is as clearly cited in prophecy as China. There is little doubt that she is "Gog, of the land of Magog." Ezekiel 38 and 39 give a clear picture of what her role will be. She will lead, supply, and encourage other nations to rebel against God and his people. Gog and Magog are the scriptural symbols of national rejection and rebellion against God.

Russia will be an enemy of Israel—she is that now. Her satellite countries, who are also mentioned in Ezekiel, will align themselves against Israel with Egypt and the Arab nations. This is happening now. Russia will supply leadership and arms to these countries; this is also being done now.

As the Jews come pouring back to Israel they will bring not only money but technical know-how. She will become rich and influential. She is discovering vital resources in the Dead Sea and under the desert.

Suddenly **Russia** will see Israel as easy prey and a rich satellite for her orbit. Ezekiel describes it this way: "Thus says the Lord God; on that day, when my people Israel are dwelling in security, you will bestir yourself and come from your place out of the far north, you and many peoples with you, all of them riding on horses, a great host and a mighty army; and you will come against my people Israel like a cloud covering the land. It will be in the latter days that I will bring you against my land, so that through you, Gog, I will vindicate my holiness before their eyes" (Ezekiel 38:14-16 Berkeley).

Poor Israel doesn't have a prayer. Or does she? God catches Russia in the mountains, and through earthquakes, landslides, floods of rain, hail, a volcano, and such confusion that they kill one another, the army is wiped out (Ezekiel 38:20-23). It will take Israel seven months to bury the dead (39:12), and the people will plunder the riches of the invaders and thus increase their wealth.

So Russia, her hatred of Israel steadily increasing, has an appointment with the God she doesn't believe exists. The hovering mountains are waiting, Gog, and you, like China, will be there on time.

Alert 20

The Jews Should Jump for Joy

The Israelis are the pivot or focal point for human history. It's a wise man who knows Jewish history in general and Jewish prophecies in particular. By being aware you can judge quite closely the end of this Age of Grace.

God has never forgotten his promises to his people, although many Jews have rejected his Son and their Messiah—Jesus. This rejection has resulted in the scattering and chastising of the nation—as also promised by the God of Abraham, Isaac and Jacob. And he promised to draw them together again.

On May 14, 1948, the "wandering Jews" became a nation again (Matthew 24:32-34). The fig tree (a symbol of Israel) blooms into life again. The once-withered Israel is again near the center of world action.

Jerusalem, the Jews' "holy city," was under Gentile (or non-Jewish) control after 586 B.C. In June 1967, this little nation took on the combined power of the surrounding Arab nations. When it was over, 100 hours later, the Jews controlled all of Jerusalem —their ancient capital.

Over 3,400 years before, God, through Moses, told the Jews what would happen to them if they rejected him. "You shall be torn away from the land you are entering to possess. The Lord will scatter you among all peoples, from one end of the earth to the other; and there you shall serve other gods of wood and stone, who have no ears, nor shall you find a resting place for the sole of your foot" (Deuteronomy 28:63-65).

But God promised to bring them back to their land and restore their prosperity when they turned back to him in repentance (30:1-5). They have not yet repented as a nation and sought God's leadership, but they are back in the land where God will again deal with them supernaturally as a people of destiny.

Some ask, "Why did God choose the Jews? They have broken every covenant God made with them." Yes, they had the mightiest leaders who ever walked the earth, and still they chose to worship idols. "What a bunch of losers!"

True! But who would have done better? We're all like our grandfather Adam, who first rejected God's way. To rescue mankind, God needed a group of people to receive and communicate his saving truth.

He wanted a nation through whom he could demonstrate his ways and send his Son. Though the Jews as a nation failed God, individual Jews gave us the only reliable revelation we have about God—the Bible—and the only Man who lived as God wanted him to—Jesus Christ. So as the Apostle Paul reminds us, Gentiles owe a great debt to the Jews.

God also chose a special people to demonstrate how greatly we need him. The Jews, despite God's special favors to them and their own wisdom, works, and wiles, blew it! They—and the rest of mankind—simply cannot make the grade in heaven without turning over their lives to God on earth.

In Luke 21:24, we read of the "times of the Gentiles," lasting until Jerusalem is finally freed from foreign domination. Israel and Jerusalem have begun to break Gentile control, but we are told that the Antichrist will proclaim himself "god" from the temple in Jerusalem (Matthew 24:15; Daniel 9:27), so Israel is not yet home free.

But to individual Jews—and non-Jews—the "times of the Gentiles" have great significance. According to the *Wycliffe Bible Commentary,* that phrase implies that "God has scheduled a day of opportunity for the Gentiles, which will close with Israel's future restoration to favor." When the "chosen people" rejected their spiritual inheritance, God chose another people — the Church — making individual believers his sons, brothers together in Christ, and living temples of the Holy Spirit! (Galatians 3:26-28; Ephesians 2:22)

Alert 21

Dem Dry Bones Are Troublemakers

We've all heard the spiritual about the "foot bone connected to the ankle bone," etc. and "dem bones walkin' around." Well, it's happening! In Ezekiel 37 we read about a valley of dry, parched bones. The Lord asks Ezekiel if he thinks those bones can live, and the prophet says, "Lord God, thou knowest." (How's that for a diplomatic cop-out?)

So the Lord says he will get them all together and put muscles on them, then skin, and finally give them breath. I can imagine Ezekiel looking out over that pile of baked bones and saying, "Right on, Lord!" But in his mind he's doubting: "No way!"

What a racket when all those bones came whipping together! They had more skeletons than a medical school! And all the time the Lord has Ezekiel giving the commands. First he has to speak right to the bones (verse 4). Again he speaks to the wind, and the bones stood, a living army (verses 9, 10). The Lord God explains the miracle in verse 11:

"Son of man, these bones are the whole house of Israel."

The phenomenon of Israel's return to nationhood has taken place in our generation. Now her troubles as a people will become the troubles of other nations who deal with her. Many have said the Near East situation is the "powderkeg" of the world that could set off World War III. Israel is destined to affect the nations of the world, as predicted in Zechariah 12:2—"This is the fate of Israel, as pronounced by the Lord: Behold, I will make Jerusalem and Judah like a cup of poison to all the nearby nations that send their armies to surround Jerusalem. Jerusalem will be a heavy stone burdening the world."

The Case of the Rising Temple

The picture of the end times—especially Israel's part—is like a magnetic puzzle with the pieces sliding together in an amazing way as Christ's coming nears.

The temple is very important in the events of the last days. I think it may not be completed before Jesus comes for his people, but I believe Christians will see renewed interest by the Jews in rebuilding the center of their worship.

There is some difference of opinion as to where the new temple would be built in Jerusalem. Zionist or politically oriented Jews couldn't care less about the religious sensibilities of the Orthodox group who feel the rebuilding of the temple is imperative. These groups may hassle more and more when it comes to the location of the construction.

The former temples were built on Mount Moriah in Jerusalem—where Abraham prepared to offer Isaac (Genesis 22:2). But today a Moslem holy place, the Dome of the Rock, occupies the site of the old temple. How it will be removed is anybody's guess—but it may be by earthquake or a war rocket.

Alert 23

Horns of Plenty-Trouble

One of the clearest alerts of all is sounded in
Daniel 7:23, 24a. "This fourth animal is the fourth
world power that will rule the earth. It will be
more brutal than any of the others; it will devour
the whole world, destroying everything before it.
His ten horns are ten kings that will rise out of
his empire."

According to Daniel's visions described in chapters 2, 7, 8, this "fourth animal" represents the last
world power before Jesus returns to establish his
perfect kingdom. Ten "horns" or kings make up
that world power, and this federation of nations
covers the same territory that made up the Roman
Empire in the Messiah's first visit to earth (9:26).

France, Italy, Belgium, Luxembourg, West
Germany, and The Netherlands are being joined
in an economic union by Britain, Ireland, Norway
and Denmark. Begun several years ago, the European Common Market is the first step toward full
partnership—under membership in the Treaty of
Rome!

Dr. Walter Hallstein, former president of the European Economic Community, stated: "Three phases of the European unification are to be noted. First, the custom union—what we have created on the way to uniting Europe is a mighty economic, political union of which nothing may be sacrificed for any reason. Its value exists not only in what it is, but more in what it promises to become—at about 1980, we may fully expect the great fusion of all economic, military, and political communities together into the United States of Europe."

In an American news magazine article, entitled "Europe's Dreams of Unity Revive," the following statement is made. "Should all go according to the most optimistic schedules, the Common Market could someday expand into a ten-nation economic entity whose industrial might would far surpass that of the Soviet Union." Now it is happening.

Out of this world power the Antichrist will come. He'll smooth his way past seven nations, but three will oppose him—and be crushed. More details on this will be given in a later chapter.

Oh, Say, Can You See . . . ?

Look quickly, because the United States of America seems doomed as a world power. The U. S. isn't mentioned clearly in prophecy, and may become a satellite of the European Common Market—if not something far worse. Let's consider some of the trends.

Crime. (Check Alert 17). The Mafia is draining our economic lifeblood. There's a tendency to make Robin Hoods of lawbreakers and label police "pigs." This deterioration of respect for law and order is a chilling omen.

Discontent. Griping and criticizing are going universal — with some justification. The kids are ripping off the establishment. People don't trust the long-hairs. Government suspects the media. Employees scheme against employers. We are tearing each other apart while our enemies watch.

Degradation. Professor Sorokin put it best: "Moral decay sets dying forces loose. We sink deeper and deeper, crying, 'I'm free.'"

Inflation. The cost of living rises steadily, while

more and more people go on public dole. How long can this go on?

Taxes. Taxes keep rising—and so do demands on public funds. Politicians say we'll have fewer schools, policemen, doctors, and so on, if taxes are cut. Then we have more dropouts, more crime, more pollution, and . . .?

Unions. These organized groups of workers are now so powerful that if a few of them called a strike, this country would be paralyzed. If the strike continued long, roving bands would plunder stores and houses to stay alive and feed their families.

Drugs and alcohol. The social cop-outs are reaching epidemic proportions. Affluence, automation, and urbanization are bringing out the worst in man. The millions of alcoholics in the United States are pathetic evidence of man's failure to live with himself.

Education. Our moral and social decline has accelerated with the court decisions to remove religious expression from public schools. I speak in many schools, and some principals admit: "We've got more pregnancies, more vandalism, more drugs, more disrespect—we need help!"

Foreign policy. We will never recover from Vietnam. Foreign respect and trust is sorely strained. President Nixon offered Iran five million dollars for a three-million-dollar narcotics crop, and was turned down because it didn't want to be a United States "lackey." Quite honestly, we are an incalculable distance from being "one nation, under God, indivisible. . . ."

Follow the Leader

Before Jesus comes to take his people to heaven, there is going to be such a dearth of strong leadership that the world will be longing for someone to follow. Certainly there is no one in the power today who commands the admiration and respect of the nations—and the need will become increasingly desperate and obvious.

The one who will eventually be revealed as Antichrist may soon begin to woo the support of nations. Or he may suddenly emerge on the world scene. He will no doubt have great influence among the ten-nation confederacy mentioned in Alert 23.

His recovery from a fatal wound during the Tribulation will secure his acceptance as world leader! "I saw that one of his heads seemed wounded beyond recovery—but the fatal wound was healed! All the world marveled at this miracle and followed the creature in awe" (Revelation 13:3).

Alert 26

It Looks Like Rain

Can't you imagine the people of Noah's day who heard him warning the populace of God's coming judgment—then watched him build a ship on dry land? Maybe it went something like this.

"Let's pack a lunch and go watch old Noah and his funny family. You won't believe his reasons for acting so strangely. When we get there you ask him yourself. It's really a riot. . . ."

"Hey, Noah! What's with this weird thing you're building?"

"Haven't you heard?" answers Noah patiently, "The Lord God is sick of your sin and idol worship. He sent me to warn you of his punishment."

"So what's he going to do to us naughty folks, Noah?"

"He's going to cover the earth with water, man; that's why I'm building this boat!"

"Wow, Noah, that's really far out. Haven't you got anything better to do with your time? We're doing OK; things aren't all bad. We haven't had as many riots. Nobody I know is starving. I go to church occasionally. The war is almost over. Wages are high. Crops are good. My daughter is marrying an ecologist next week. And the company is throwing a big party in Vegas. . . . Poor Noah; never has any fun. Oh, well, I guess we'll always have fanatics around."

"Yeah! Hurry up, though, *it looks like rain!*"

"The world will be at ease—banquets and parties and weddings—just as it was in Noah's time before the sudden coming of the flood; people wouldn't believe what was going to happen until the flood actually arrived and took them all away. So shall my coming be" (Matthew 24:37, 38).

The world says things are improving. God says they'll get worse.

Biblical illiterates say peace among nations is possible. God says nations will rise against nations and there will be wars.

Scientific man says he will overcome the problems of disease and famine. God says they will increase.

Secular man plans to revise, construct, educate, revitalize, clean up, change administrations, innovate, improve, allocate, and cut back until he can find the right combination for peace, security, and universal satisfaction. The Christian reads his Bible with the eyes of faith and understands the signs of today and the future.

Big storm ahead—and sunshine above the clouds!

The Jesus Revolution

The tidal wave of interest in Jesus is surging from coast to coast. This is not just a fad or rebound from the drug culture or rebellion's failure. This is a movement that is growing up.

The "Jesus People" have endured the publicity that punctures many colorful balloons. The good has overcome the questionable and weak aspects magnified by critics. Real, honest love is blunting the barbs.

I have seen this for myself. Their concern for others is genuine. Ordinary Christians have played it cool so long that a display of "I love you, and I'll help you regardless of the cost or who's looking" is very hard to handle.

More important, they may be a part of the prophecy of Jesus' coming. I think they are the "children of Joel," the ones he mentions in Joel 2:28—"I will pour out of my Spirit upon all of you! Your sons and daughters will prophesy; your old men will dream dreams, and your young men see visions. . . ."

You Can Help It Happen

Paul said, "In the last days it will be difficult to be a Christian." Some of the reasons he gave in 2 Timothy 3:1-5 are:

People will love only themselves and their money;

they will be proud and boastful;

they'll sneer at God;

they'll be disobedient to parents, ungrateful to them, and thoroughly bad.

they will be hardheaded and never give in to others;

they will be constant liars and troublemakers;

they will think nothing of immorality;

they will be rough and cruel;

they'll sneer at those who try to be good;

they will betray their friends;

they'll be hot-headed;

they will be puffed up with pride;

they will prefer good times to worshiping God;

they will go to church, yes, but they won't really

believe anything they hear.

So what can we do?

We can understand God's great plan and have a part in the success of it. His program will get done—and on time—and he'll use whoever wants a part of this eternal action badly enough to move out. You have to let it cost you. Invest your life today in the sure and fantastic rewards of his future.

"He isn't really being slow about his promised return, even though it sometimes seems that way. But he is waiting, for the good reason that he is not willing that any should perish, and he is giving more time for sinners to repent. The day of the Lord is surely coming, as unexpectedly as a thief. . . . You should look forward to that day and hurry it along. . . . And remember why he is waiting. He is giving us time to get his message of salvation out to others" (2 Peter, 3:9, 10a, 12a, 15a).

2

UP, UP AND AWAY

International storm signals are whipping ominously in the hurricane of world events. Something *big* is hovering near. The "Global Village" predicted by today's planners may soon be a fact—but with Antichrist as world mayor. When that happens, tyranny will become worldwide and the terrible events of the Great Tribulation will erupt. That will be a payoff time: destruction and death for Christ-rejectors; and rescue and rejoicing for Christ-lovers.

Christians will be delivered from the horrors of

the Tribulation by Christ's rescue of his people, called the Rapture. The Apostle Paul describes it like this:

First, the Dead

"I can tell you this directly from the Lord: That we who are still living when the Lord returns will not rise to meet him ahead of those who are in their graves. For the Lord himself will come down from heaven with a mighty shout and the soul-stirring cry of the archangel and the great trumpet-call of God. And the Christians who are dead will be the first to rise to meet the Lord. Then we who are still alive and remain on the earth will be caught up with them in the clouds to meet the Lord in the air and remain with him forever. So comfort and encourage one another with this news" (1 Thessalonians 4:15-18).

Let's check out "those who are in their graves." I'm often asked, "Where do Christians go when they die?"

Their bodies go to the grave, like anyone else's, there to await Christ's resurrection signal at the Rapture. The Christian's spirit joins Christ at the time of physical death, as Paul indicated in Philippians 1:23. When the resurrected body rejoins its spirit, the fullness of life in eternity will begin.

The spirits of departed unbelievers, meanwhile, are in hades, a stopover point on the way to the eternal lake of fire (Revelation 20:13-15). Jesus himself described the conditions in hades. He used the name of the man who went to paradise instead of hades, so we believe this was an actual happening, not just an illustration.

"Finally the beggar [Lazarus] died and was carried by the angels to be with Abraham in the place of the righteous dead. The rich man also died and was buried, and his soul went into hades. There, in torment, he saw Lazarus in the far distance with Abraham. 'Father Abraham,' he shouted, 'have some pity! Send Lazarus over if only to dip the tip of his finger in water and cool my tongue for I am in anguish in these flames' " (Luke 16:22-24).

No one could help the once-wealthy man because a chasm surrounded hades and it was uncrossable except by doomed souls on their way in. There's no exit from hell!

Then the Living

The shout of Jesus—a shout of joy—summons earth's Christians to their tryst in the sky. We are his bride, his blood-bought possession, and he's coming to take us home. The archangel peals a cry of victory in the language of the soul, confirming our faith and hope in our heavenly destiny. And the trumpet of God splits the sky—though only those on the right frequency will hear the call. John put it like this in Revelation 4:1: "Then as I looked, I saw a door standing open in heaven, and the same voice I had heard before, that sounded like a mighty trumpet blast, spoke to me and said, 'Come up here and I will show you what must happen in the future.' "

We, too, are going to hear this and discover "in

the twinkling of an eye" that gravity has no more control over us. Our bodies are changed and the pressures of "speed-of-light" travel won't affect us at all. It will be all over down here—for us.

Jesus Face to Face

Jesus will be *parousia, apokalupsis,* and *epiphaneia.* If that's all Greek to you, welcome to the club. But hang in there. When you learn the meaning of these words, you'll be glad you did.

Jesus will be *parousia*—with us in a form like ours. It means "to be near or alongside," so at his coming we'll know him and sense him near—realizing he came just for us. As he became our *personal* Savior, so he wants us to understand that he will be *parousia*—personal Redeemer (1 Thessalonians 2:19).

Jesus will be *apokalupsis*—his overpowering glory will blaze around us—and we will not die. The full impact of who he is and what he gave up to become our Savior will be revealed; the stunning unveiling of his deity will so captivate us that we will worship in adoration. The *apokalupsis* also refers to our majestic return with him at the end of the Tribulation. "And when Christ who is our real life comes back again, you will shine with him and share in all his glories" (Colossians 3:4).

Jesus will be *epiphaneia*—totally manifested. The great mystery of Jesus' combined humanity and deity will be understood. The world has denied his deity because it lacked the faith to accept what it did not understand. No faith is required to believe in "Jesus Christ Superstar." But faith changes the human "Superstar" into a divine and personal Savior.

Roman rulers tried to deify themselves, and although the people pretended to believe, they mocked their inconsistency and failure at trying to be gods. Then Jesus came. He was God-man. They tried to prove him sinful and couldn't, tempted him and failed, tortured him and he took it silently. They couldn't even kill him, really, because he gave his life (John 10:18). Mere men could not kill the Son of God!

Epiphaneia! We will fully know Jesus!

Who's Going to Be Here?

Some Christians do not expect to escape the terrors of the Tribulation. They anticipate Jesus' return, but not before Christians have suffered with others the plagues that are due to break over the earth. But that prospect doesn't sound like the "blessed hope" of Titus 2:13 that I anticipate. The Church of Christ has a far different life than unbelievers both in this world and the world to come. Perhaps we need to clarify who the Church is.

The Church, the bride, and the body of Christ are all terms for people who have received Jesus Christ by faith as personal Savior and Lord. This, of course, does not include all church-goers. People who believe facts about God, Jesus, and the Holy Spirit; who recite the Apostles Creed; who may have been baptized and confirmed are not necessarily members of Christ's Church. There is a dramatic difference between intellectual and heart belief. I can believe in a doctor's reputation, but if I don't take the medicine he prescribes I don't really trust him—I am not entrusting my health to his diagnosis. It could cost me my life and I would deserve to be called a dead fool.

So it is with the Great Physician, Jesus. "But to all who received him, he gave the right to become the children of God. All they needed to do was to trust him to save them" (John 1:12). Notice the word "received." So many "believe" certain facts and are church members but they have not *received* Jesus Christ because they have not believed him from their heart and consequently obeyed him in their life (Romans 6:17). Only those in the spiritual Church will be raptured to meet Jesus. Will you be there—instead of in the midst of the awful Tribulation on earth?

The Tribulation is divine wrath and judgment sent against the wicked individuals and nations of the earth who have rejected God's only and last hope, his Son, Jesus (Revelation 10:19; 11:18; 14:8; 15:1, 7; 16:1). Jesus bore the judgment of sinners who trust him when he died on the cross (1 Peter 2:24). As a result, "God appointed us not unto wrath, but unto the obtaining of salvation through our Lord Jesus Christ" (1 Thessalonians 5:9). "So there is now no condemnation awaiting those who belong to Christ Jesus" (Romans 8:1). A promise to the waiting Church appears in Revelation 3:10—"Because you have patiently obeyed me despite the persecution, therefore I will protect you from the time of Great Tribulation and temptation, which will come upon the world to test everyone alive."

The word that makes the difference is "from." In six translations, The Living Bible, Amplified, Berkeley, King James, Revised Standard, and Phillips, each gave the word "from," not "through" or "during" or "in" the Tribulation. Scholars Thiessen and Thayer show the difference between the Greek prepositions *en* and *ek*. *Entered* means "to cause one to persevere or stand firm in a thing"; *ektered* means "to cause one to escape in safety out of." The preposition used here was *ek*. We're going to be up and away from the "time of Jacob's trouble."

In 2 Peter 2:6-9 Lot is called a righteous man. This sheds light on Genesis 19:22, where the angel sought to hasten the departure of Lot with the words, "Hurry and escape to Zoar, for I can do nothing until you have reached it." If the presence of one righteous man prevented the outpouring of deserved judgment on the city of Sodom, it seems logically consistent that the presence of the Church, Christ's beloved bride, would prevent the outpouring of divine wrath until she is removed.

Finally, not once is the Great Tribulation even mentioned in the Epistles, the books especially written for the Church. Reason? We're not going to be here; so no instructions were necessary.

What Now?

If you had to appear before a judges' stand,

would you rather be sentenced by a court of law or receive a prize after competing in a race? Your answer probably didn't cause any brain strain, right? We all like to be rewarded, not sentenced. But the word "reward" does have a double meaning, such as "the just reward of the wicked" and "the rewards of the Christian." Our swift ascension to meet Jesus in the air is the beginning of our rewards.

Then we appear before the *Bema,* another Greek word that means "reward," not "judgment." We will not be judged as to our right to be there, since God promised: "Their sins and iniquities will I remember no more" (Hebrews 10:17). We will be examined for our works—"the things we've done in our earthly bodies" (2 Corinthians 5:10).

Paul told us: "For no one can ever lay any other foundation than that one we already have—Jesus Christ," but Christians can use various kinds of materials to build on that foundation. Some use love and sacrifice and righteousness—like gold and silver and jewels in quality; and some careless Christians build with pride, reputation, and hypocrisy—sticks, hay, and straw! Every Christian's work will be put through "fire" to show its real condition. Every workman who has built with the right materials will receive his pay—rewards from the Master Builder. But if the house he has built burns up, the Christian will be saved, "but like a man escaping through a wall of flames" (1 Corinthians 3:11-15). There is still building time!

The Fire Falls

There are our works—all of them. If the examination were based on external evidence, some of us could pile up an impressive mountain of good things done. But the truth is, we're going to be checked for our motives and faith. How much was done in the power of and for the glory of self? How much was done out of habit? (Church attendance can be just that.) How many people are present every time the church door is open, but are critical, dried-up, and unloving, thinking they're "chalking up points" by showing up?

I've found myself checking my motives and examining my actions: Has my service been free of selfishness and pride? This hung me up for awhile, then I realized that the very fact I was concerned was a good check. And to do less so there would be less risk of wrong motives would be a phony escape and contrary to God's will. The devil would like that. So you and I will have to trust the Holy Spirit within us to interpret God's will to us and help us do it with all our hearts. Don't forget, God rewards us for our faithfulness—not our success as man sees it.

One of my heroes had a few thoughts on this matter. His name is Paul, and spiritually he had it together like few men ever have. He said, "I run the race with determination. I am no shadow boxer; I really fight! I am my body's sternest master, for fear that when I have preached to others I should myself be disqualified (1 Corinthians 9:26, 27, Phil-

lips). He kept checking his motives and resisting
temptation so he wouldn't lose his reward. (This
didn't affect his salvation, as 1 Corinthians 3:15
shows.)

Order Your Crown Now

Only a few of the elite people on earth have
crowns—and often they are inherited, not earned.
All Christians have the opportunity of gaining
crowns in heaven which will indicate spiritual merit.

1. *The Incorruptible Crown* is for those who have
gained mastery over their sinful nature (1 Corinthians 9:25). You've got to fight for this one! Stay
on the track, and keep running; remember that the
Christian life isn't a sprint, it's a marathon. Make
sure you're running when he comes.

2. *The Crown of Rejoicing* is for soul-winners (1
Thessalonians 2:19). Don't wait around for a special commission: look around and see the opportu-
nities God has arranged for you.

3. *The Crown of Life* is for those who endure
temptation. "Happy is the man who doesn't give in
and do wrong when he is tempted, for afterward
he will get as his reward the crown of life that God
has promised those that love him" (James 1:12).

4. *The Crown of Righteousness* is for Christians
eagerly awaiting the return of Christ (2 Timothy
4:8). If this book helps you to look for and love his
reappearing, then we'll both wear this crown.

5. *The Crown of Glory* is for those whose lives
are devoted to serving him, who "feed the flock"
of God (1 Peter 5:4). This appears to be one of

the worthiest crowns—perhaps because it's so costly to gain!

I believe the crowns will give us great joy, but we'll want to give them in worship and thanksgiving to the one who enabled us to win them, our Savior and Lord.

The Wedding

As we've seen, the true Church and Christ are described in the New Testament as the bride and Bridegroom. The pure bride is now fully prepared to be presented to Christ, "clothed upon with righteousness." The jubilant wedding scene is glimpsed by John in Revelation 19:7, 8—"Let us be glad and rejoice and honor him, for the time has come for the wedding banquet of the Lamb, and his bride has prepared herself. She is permitted to wear the cleanest and whitest and finest of linens."

Now God the Father achieves the purpose of his creation and redemption of humanity as he "presents us faultless before the presence of his glory with exceeding joy" (Jude 24). The spiritual union is complete, and we are one in Jesus Christ. Only the actual event will reveal the sublime joys of this royal relationship.

3

2,555 DAYS OF BAD NEWS

Imagine, if you can, the scene on earth when a few million people disappear in the rapturing of the Church.

A high jumper approaches the bar and takes off—to a new world record—man, he never came down! "Out of sight," murmurs a bewildered spectator in the understatement of the century.

A husband who couldn't stand his wife's nagging him to "accept Christ" won't be bothered any more; she's gone—for good!

The sophisticated college skeptic enrolls in a "Witchcraft" course to find out what happened to his missing roommate.

The pastor who never told his people that Jesus is the only "Way, the Truth, and the Life," and that he is coming again will have a church full of Tribulation-bound people wanting explanations.

The professors of religion who derided the Bible and philosophers who mocked religious faith will be out of jobs—unless they're willing to be hired priests for the new religion of man.

Teen-agers who refused the faith of their square Christian parents will find themselves orphans in a hostile, uptight world. Their friends will betray them to save their own skin.

Wrath

After the shock of this fantastic event, the word "wrath" will describe the years to follow. As hard as it may be to believe, men will despise God and blame him for "not giving them a chance." Those who should have learned the truth will be raging rebels against God. They will believe lies with all their hearts. Paul describes their fate.

"As for the work this man of rebellion and hell will do when he comes, it is already going on, but he himself will not come until the one who is holding him back steps out of the way. Then this wicked one will appear, whom the Lord Jesus will burn up with the breath of his mouth and destroy by his presence when he returns. This man of sin shall come as Satan's tool, full of satanic power, and will do great miracles. He will completely fool those who are on their way to hell because they have said 'no' to the truth; they have refused to believe it and love it, and let it save them, so God will allow them to believe lies with all their hearts. And all of them will be justly judged for believing falsehood, refusing the truth, and enjoying their sins" (2 Thessalonians 2:7-12).

The wrath of men (Revelation 11:18), the wrath of Satan against Israel (Revelation 12), and the wrath of Satan's puppet—the "Beast"—against those who believe (Revelation 13:7) will be terrible. But all their wrath cannot be compared to the wrath of God against a world that has constantly defied and disobeyed him.

Eating forbidden fruit in the Garden of Eden, refusing to worship as directed, killing God's messengers, praying to idols, wallowing in immorality, killing the Son of God, persecuting the helpless, martyring hosts of saints, desecrating the Bible, blaspheming the Holy Ghost—the wickedness mounts up to heaven and overflows to hell. The age of opportunity is ended and God's wrath thunders down.

"And they said to the mountains and rocks, fall on us, and hide us from the face of him that sits on the throne, and from the wrath of the Lamb; for the great day of his wrath is come; and who shall be able to stand?" (Revelation 6:16, 17).

Wrath Plus Mercy Equals Hope

Even in the heat of God's wrath, his mercy is evident. He has not forgotten his people Israel and his promises to them. He is using the Tribulation to bring about the conversion of a multitude of Jews and prepare the nation Israel to welcome their Messiah. Their King will indeed return, and this time he will make Jerusalem the capital of the world.

Revelation 7:1-3 describes four angels poised at four points on the earth, ready to unleash havoc. As mercy was offered before judgment struck in Egypt, Sodom, and the world of Noah, God will again broadcast the message of his love and forgiveness to those who will listen.

144,000 Jews Get It On

The world is going to "get the word" as never before. The word "fanatic" has hardly been illustrated until these Jesus-is-Messiah evangelists take on the world. They'll have money and means to get out the good news and they won't waste time. Revelation 7:9-14 describes those they win to Christ and says they can't be numbered. Notice they come from "all nations and provinces and languages." So the final fulfillment of Matthew 24:14 will be realized: "And the good news about the kingdom will be preached throughout the whole world, so that all nations will hear it, and then, finally, the end will come."

Evangelist-author Lehman Strauss makes this comment in *The Book of the Revelation,* published by Loizeaux Brothers: "The 144,000 witnessing Israelites will be persecuted for their testimony. They will be hungry, thirsty, lonely, in need of clothing and cast into prison. But those Gentiles who believe their message will stand with them and minister to them, so that it is to them Jesus will say, 'When you did it unto these my brothers, you were doing it unto me!' " (Matthew 25:40).

There are various interpretations today about the identity of these 144,000. If someone tries to tell you their sect or group is the chosen 144,000, ask what Jewish tribe they belong to. For these are plainly all Jews from the twelve tribes of Israel. The list is in Revelation 7.

An interesting fact is that the tribe of Dan is not included in that list. This family engaged in deep idolatry (Judges 18), and Dan's descendants are not permitted representation. Instead of Dan, Joseph's son Manasseh is included.

The 144,000 are sealed with "the seal of the living God." This means they will be given a mark in their foreheads (Revelation 7:3, 4) to identify them as God's people, just as those who worship the Beast will be marked with his number. They will be miraculously preserved as witnesses until their mission is completed.

Revelation 7:14-17 presents the heavenly scene that follows the evangelists' worldwide campaign. " 'These are the ones coming out of the Great Tribulation,' he said; 'they washed their robes and whitened them by the blood of the Lamb. That is why they are here before the throne of God, serving him day and night in his temple. The one sitting on the throne will shelter them; they will never be hungry again, nor thirsty, and they will be fully protected from the scorching noontime heat. For the

Lamb standing in front of the throne will feed them
and be their Shepherd and lead them to the springs
of the water of life. And God shall wipe their tears
away.' "

The Dynamic Duo

Now we come to one of the most fascinating sit-
uations of the Tribulation period. To set the stage,
we'll first explain that the Antichrist probably has
not yet taken over the world, but operating through
the ten-nation confederacy he has made a treaty
with Israel. He allows Israel to restore her temple
sacrifices, as in Old Testament times. He displays
amazing diplomacy in bringing peace and settling
misunderstandings (Daniel 8:25). The world is get-
ting to know him and admire him.

Suddenly two men make their appearance in
Jerusalem (Revelation 11:3-13). They will go to the
important places of influence and repudiate the
Antichrist. They'll tell the world of God's coming
judgment and confirm their words with miracles.
They will be feared and hated by the religious and
political leaders who are scheming for mastery and
wealth. Who are these men?

I am convinced that one is Elijah. Here are some
of the reasons.

1. Malachi predicted Elijah would come to prepare the way for the Messiah (Malachi 3:1-3; 4:5,
6). Don't confuse this with the Rapture, the return
of Christ to the clouds for his people. This coming
relates to "the great and dreadful day of the Lord"
at the end of the Tribulation.

2. Elijah didn't die (2 Kings 2:9-11), so he already has a transformed spiritual body.

3. Elijah was one of the two men from heaven who appeared to Jesus and his disciples at the Savior's transfiguration (Matthew 17:1-3).

The second witness is not so easy to identify. Some think it will be Moses because he appeared with Elijah at the transfiguration. We have an account of his death in Deuteronomy 34:5. Moses had the distinction of being buried by God. The only other man we know of who didn't die was Enoch (the man who "walked with God"). I believe Enoch will be Elijah's partner in power. Enoch was a prophet of judgment to Israel, as was Elijah (Jude 14, 15). And this is their ministry during the Tribulation.

Regardless, the dynamic duo are on earth to remind unbelieving men of judgment. While 144,000 witnesses call men to accept Christ, these two demonstrate the high price of evil. Their first move is to shut off the rain. For three and one-half years, the whole time they are on earth, not one drop of rain falls. They also have power to turn rivers blood-red with impurities.

Imagine scientists' frustration when their attempts to supply water are thwarted by the two witnesses. It will be useless to file protests to the authorities. No one can control these ambassadors from heaven who are commissioned to make human life miserable and turn men to God. They send waves of disease and plagues across the earth, perhaps similar to the plagues that Moses brought against Egypt.

Darkness—so black it can be felt. Flying insects—with stings like those of scorpions. Terrible pain—and no relief. J. J. Van Gorder speculated: "It may be that suffering men will plunge into lakes or seas to seek death by drowning, only to find for some unknown reason that their bodies will not sink. Poison may be swallowed only to find it has been neutralized to impotency" *(Things to Come,* by J. Dwight Pentecost, Dunham Publishing Co.).

One thing is sure: men will hate the two prophets of judgment and feel they would do the world a favor by killing them. Imagine the reward to anyone who can kill them. But that's not an easy task, and the bodies of those who try will be mute evidence. Revelation 11:5 tells why: "Anyone trying to harm them will be killed by bursts of fire shooting out of their mouths." God calls them "my witnesses," and that means no one can harm them until their work is done.

But after three and one-half years their witness is finished, and the Beast kills them. This, of course, will add to his already immense popularity. He now takes every advantage, political and social, and leaves their bodies in the streets of Jerusalem for three and one-half days. "No one will be allowed to bury them. And people from many nations will crowd around to gaze at them. And there will be a worldwide holiday. People everywhere will rejoice and give presents to each other and throw parties to celebrate the death of the two prophets who had tormented them so much" (Revelation

11:9, 10). The communication satellites in orbit will feature their deaths to the world.

We see here the total degeneration and perversion of men. They have completely reversed moral standards: wrong is right to them. Their hearts are set against God and like clay for the Antichrist to mold.

Imagine a great crowd gathered to honor the mighty one who delivered the world from the scourge of the prophets. Television is carrying the final celebration of their deaths before the Antichrist orders their bodies destroyed. While he is giving a great speech exalting himself and blaspheming God, the arm of Elijah twitches and his eyes open. Suddenly the crowd goes silent. They watch in horror and fear. Elijah, then Enoch, rise to their feet. With blazing eyes they gaze into the lens of the cameras. Then they both focus on the evil prince of hell and finally they look up. "And a loud voice will shout from heaven, 'Come up!' And they will rise to heaven in a cloud as their enemies watch" (Revelation 11:12). Realizing the effect this will have on the world, the Antichrist screams his feeble explanations but his voice is drowned out by the roar of an earthquake (11:13). A tenth of Jerusalem is reduced to rubble and 7,000 men lie dead. One scholar says this means: "7,000 'name' men or men of distinction lie dead." The observers in Jerusalem can discern this "sign." "Then everyone left will, in their terror, give glory to God."

But the Antichrist is just beginning his terror

reign. He sells out to Satan and receives fantastic powers to back up his political and natural abilities. Satan will walk the earth in the person of this demonized man. From now on we'll refer to him as the "Beast" instead of "Antichrist."

War in Heaven

The turmoil on earth suddenly explodes because of an epochal event in the heavens described in Revelation 12.

"Then there was war in heaven; Michael and the angels under his command fought the dragon and his hosts of fallen angels. And the dragon lost the battle and was forced from heaven. This great dragon—the ancient serpent called the devil, or Satan, the one deceiving the whole world—was thrown down unto the earth with all his army.

"Then I heard a voice shouting across the heavens, 'It has happened at last! God's salvation and the power and the rule, and the authority of his Christ are finally here. For the accuser of our brothers has been thrown down from heaven unto the earth—he accused them day and night before our God. . . . Rejoice, O heavens! You citizens of heaven, rejoice! Be glad! But woe to you people of the world, for the devil has come down to you in great anger, knowing that he has little time.' And when the devil found himself cast down to earth, he persecuted the woman who had given birth to the child" (12:7-10, 12, 13).

The devil has beeen at war with God's Son ever since the Garden of Eden. His purpose has always

been to block man's reunion with God. His diabolical attempts included the deception of Adam and
Eve; the murder of Abel by Cain; King Herod's
decree to slaughter boy babies of Jesus' age; attack
by infuriated mobs trying to kill Jesus; Satan's offer
of the world to Jesus in exchange for allegiance.

Satan failed, but he did not give up. For some
reason, God allowed him continued access to
heaven where he insidiously accused *you and me* for
our failures. For example: "Look at that phony
Christian down there. He attends church and fakes
out everyone there, but look at these vile thoughts
in his mind this week. And he cheated too. . . ."
Sadly, he's right in some of these accusations. But
you and I are not defenseless.

Jesus stands and pleads our case before the
Father. "It's true they fail, but some have asked
forgiveness in my name, and the Holy Spirit is
dealing with others. For my sake, Father, be patient
with them, for they are mine." And the accuser
is repulsed again.

The beginning of the end for Satan arrives when
God gives power to Michael and his angels to force
Satan and his demons out of heaven (Revelation
12:9). So the "Prince of the power of the air," as
Satan is called in Ephesians 2:2, is humiliatingly
catapulted to earth.

Now he knows his time is limited. In unbelievable fury he turns on Israel—the "woman" of Revelation 12—who produced Jesus, the God-Man.
Satan hates these people who have been God's
channel of special blessings to mankind.

But Satan, a spirit, needs a man to enact his final plans and bring "the time of Jacob's trouble" upon Israel (Jeremiah 30:7). There will be such a man, aching to sell his soul for power to rule the world.

The Devil's Disciple

"He will defy the most high God, and wear down the saints with persecution, and try to change all laws, morals, and customs. God's people will be helpless in his hands for three and one-half years" (Daniel 7:25). "Then the dragon (Satan) encouraged the beast to speak great blasphemies against the Lord; and gave him authority to control the earth for forty-two months. All that time he blasphemed God's name and his temple and all those living in heaven. The dragon gave him power to fight against God's people and to overcome them, and to rule over all nations and language groups throughout the world" (Revelation 13:5-7).

Let's take a close look at this beast-man. Revelation 13:3 says the "world followed the Creature in awe!" There are good reasons for this. The greatest is that they are convinced they have finally found a man who has cheated death. Revelation 13:3, 12, 14 mention the fatal head wound of the beast from which he recovers and causes the world to marvel. How strange that people who would not believe Christ rose from the dead will believe in the resurrection of this evil man!

This man who made a treaty with the Jews and helped them reestablish their temple sacrifices is now drunk with power, his mind reprogrammed by

Satan. Daniel 9:27 tells us he will enter the holy place of the temple and defile the sanctuary of God. "He will defy every God there is, and tear down every other object of adoration and worship. He will go in and sit as God in the temple of God, claiming that he himself is God (2 Thessalonians 2:4).

The Enforcer

Coming to the Beast's aid is an electrifying prime minister. He is called the "second beast." Revelation 13 tells us, "He exercised all the authority of the Creature whose death-wound had been healed, whom he required all the world to worship. And he did unbelievable miracles such as making fire flame down to earth from the skies while everyone was watching. By doing these miracles, he was deceiving people everywhere."

The miracles of this False Prophet are designed to deceive people into thinking he is Elijah. Elijah called down fire from heaven in Old Testament days as proof that he was from God (1 Kings 18:36-38). This unholy trinity—Satan, the Beast, and the False Prophet—hope to fake Israel into accepting the Beast as the Messiah!

When the False Prophet stages an international TV spectacular to demonstrate his power, the world will be watching. I can imagine the buildup. Lesser acts of black magic, fortune-telling, astrology, and immorality will precede the main event. After a dramatic speech in which he prophesies that he will make fire fall, he reaches up and—whoosh! A jet stream of fire cascades down. Gasps go up from the awestruck crowd, and around the world the miracle is on everyone's lips.

Another move is to order world citizens to send money to finance the building of a gigantic statue of the Beast. This will be built in Jerusalem, the new center of worldwide religion. Inspired by what they've seen, the countries of the world provide the money and the image is quickly erected.

Then: "Everyone is commanded to bow down and worship the image of the Beast," announces the False Prophet. "But to prove once again that the Beast is worthy of our worship, listen closely." Again the world goes silent in anticipation. Suddenly the lips of the statue begin to move and it speaks! "Bow down, people of the earth. Bow down and worship me. Honor and obey the Beast or you will die!"

This is not imagination—but the awful prophecy of Revelation 13:15.

Thousands of duplicate statues may be shipped around the world and placed on corners, in schools, churches, offices. At every public gathering all will be required to bow. When one passes an image he must bow. The old idols and superstitions of history have been superseded by the greatest, last counterfeit!

666

The False Prophet goes one step farther in his tyrannical plan. "He required everyone—great and small, rich and poor, slave and free—to be tattooed with a certain mark on the right hand or on the forehead. And no one could get a job or even buy in any store without the permit of that mark, which was either the name of the Creature or the code number of his name. . . . The numerical values of the letters in his name add to 666" (Revelation 13:16-18).

In Scripture the number six stands for man; three is God's number. Three sixes indicate man's attempt to be God. But seven is the number of perfection. Even the man who can bring the world together and perform miracles falls short of God's perfection!

We may not be far from a programmed, dictatorial system. Vast amounts of data on individuals have been collected by modern governments. A dictator would construct an immensely elaborated system to control everyone and everything. And blinded mankind will worship him—their last hope.

Historian Arnold Toynbee has read some of the signs. He said, "By forcing on mankind more and more lethal weapons, and at the same time making the world more and more interdependent economically, technology has brought mankind to such a degree of distress that we are ripe for the deifying of any new Caesar who might succeed in giving the world unity and peace" (Des Moines *Tribune,* August 8, 1971).

The stage is being set!

4

THE WRATH OF GOD

It is hard to try to correlate the three series of judgments and plagues described in the book of Revelation. To help us get an overall picture of these convulsive events, I have condensed and paraphrased the lists. These punishments sent by God add to the grief and misery caused by the tyrannical Antichrist.

The Seals—Revelation 6

First—False peace
Second—Wars; anarchy reigns
Third—Famine

Fourth—Death

Fifth—Persecution of believers

Sixth—Earthquakes; sun turns black; moon turns
      red; stars appear to fall and the starry
      heavens disappear

Seventh—Ominous quiet preceding onslaught of
      Trumpet judgments

Although the Seals begin the first judgments,
they continue throughout the Tribulation period.
The sixth Seal apparently comes near the end. The
Trumpet and Bowl judgments roar in concurrently
with the Seals.

The Trumpets—Revelation 8–10

First—Hail, fire, and blood fall; one-third of the
      trees and grass burn up

Second—One-third of ships and fish destroyed;
      one-third of sea turned to blood

Third—A falling star poisons one-third of river
      and spring water

Fourth—The sun's power reduced by one-third;
      night lights dimmed

Fifth—An army of locustlike creatures with the
      intelligence of men and sting of scorpions
      torture mankind for five months

Sixth—An army of 200 million under the leader-
      ship of four demons slaughter one-third
      of the world's population. (I believe these
      are the "kings of the East" mentioned in
      Revelation 16:12)

Seventh—Devastating earthquake; announce-
      ment of God's victory over world

The Bowls—(Vials)—Revelation 16

First—Malignant sores on people wearing the
mark of the Beast

Second—Oceans turn to blood and life in them
dies

Third—Rivers and springs become undrinkable

Fourth—Sun's heat intensifies and burns everyone

Fifth—Total darkness

Sixth—River Euphrates dries up (Now the kings
of the East can march unhindered against
the Mideast; see Sixth Trumpet)

Seventh—World's worst earthquake: islands van-
ish and mountains flatten out; 100-
pound hailstones fall

You would think suffering mankind would repent
and ask God to forgive them for their evil that
brought on these judgments, but that will not
happen!

"But the men left alive after these plagues still
refused to worship God! They would not renounce
their demon-worship, nor their idols made of gold
and silver, brass, stone, and wood—which neither
see nor hear nor walk. Neither did they change
their mind and attitude about all their murders and
witchcraft, their immorality and theft" (Revelation 9:20, 21).

"Everyone was burned by this blast of heat, and
they cursed the name of God who sent the plagues—
they did not change their mind and attitude to give
him glory" (16:9).

"And there was an incredible hailstorm from
heaven; hailstones weighing a hundred pounds fell

from the sky onto the people below, and they cursed God because of the terrible hail" (16:21).

5

DEATH OF THE
SPIRITUAL WHORE

The "Whore" described in Revelation 17 is a worldwide system of phony religions. We can see it forming in the "ecumenical movement" among Western nations and the mystical Eastern religions such as Baha'i and Theosophy. These humanistic associations imagine that mankind can save himself and please whatever God may exist, not realizing their real god is Satan.

In these movements and religions, agreement and harmony among men seem to be the greatest virtues—a peace-at-any-price philosophy which the Antichrist will heartily encourage until he exacts his awful price: worship of himself.

Is God caught off guard? Has he warned misguided mankind? Check 1 Timothy 4:1—"But the Holy Spirit tells us clearly that in the last times some in the church will turn away from Christ and become eager followers of teachers with devil-inspired ideas."

And 2 Timothy 3:5: "They will go to church, yes, but they won't really believe anything they hear. Don't be taken in by people like that."

Further, 2 Peter 2:1, 2 warns, "But there were false prophets, too, in those days, just as there will be false teachers among you. They will cleverly tell their lies about God, turning against even their master who bought them; but theirs will be a swift and terrible end. Many will follow their evil teaching that there is nothing wrong with sexual sin. And because of them Christ and his way will be scoffed at."

The Whore's name in Revelation 17 is "Babylon the Great, the Mother of Harlots and Abominations of the Earth." The reason is that the early city-state, Babylon, began the religion of man and the worship of occult powers (Genesis 10, 11; Isaiah 47). From the beginning man rebelled against God, but he was restless with no superior being to worship. Led by the evil Nimrod (Genesis 10:10), who faked the people into thinking the new concept of self-improvement was of God, the nation began building the Tower of Babel, a monument to star-worship. The ensuing confusion of languages and worldwide dispersion was God's counterattack against united wickedness.

Babylon's Last Ride

In Revelation 17:3 John describes the Whore "sitting upon a scarlet-colored Beast." This is the Antichrist we've already met. His political system is allied with this counterfeit religion. He knows people everywhere are religious and need to worship something—preferably something visible and not very demanding.

The Common Market's future headquarters will likely be in Rome. Notice in verse 9 the Whore's location: "The seven heads are the seven mountains, on which the Woman sits." Rome is called "the City of the Seven Hills"—what a coincidence! Religious direction and political control will issue from the same city.

The true nature of this evil "church" is revealed in verse 6 as "drunk with the blood of the saints and martyrs of Jesus." She will not tolerate the truth, and will stop at nothing to achieve what her blindness considers right. History records multitudes slaughtered in God's name during the Inquisition, the Crusades, and on mission fields around the world.

The spiritual Whore is riding high in Revelation 17. One reason is her great wealth. Can you imagine the combined fortune of the religious organizations in property, jewels, and art? She'll probably be investing heavily in the worldwide business ventures of future markets.

Remember the little story of the gingerbread

man? He was some kind of fast cookie! No one
could catch him until he got in over his head—so to
speak. When he came to a stream it just happened
that a sly fox was waiting and offered transporta-
tion across. He moved that poor cookie from his
tail to his head and nose—and suddenly the for-
tunes of the cookie were swallowed up.

This is what happens to the Whore, the phony
religion. "The Scarlet Animal and his ten horns—
which represent ten kings who will reign with him—
all hate the Woman, and will attack her and leave
her naked and ravaged by fire. For God will put a
plan into their minds, a plan that will carry out his
purposes. They will mutually agree to give their
authority to the Scarlet Animal, so that the words
of God will be fulfilled. And this Woman you saw
in your vision represents the great city that rules
over the kings of the earth" (Revelation 17:16-18).

So the final judgment of God against man-
oriented religion is meted out by man—with hatred.
The federated nations realize they've been used
and are sick of it; their wrath is so intense that they
destroy her completely. Once again God uses "the
wrath of men to praise him."

Since the Whore is deeply involved in commerce
and politics, her destruction will shake these foundations also. God's judgments are always complete.
Revelation 18 tells of an angel who comes and
announces the downfall of the Whore, here called
"Babylon." The religion which deceived people
into believing it was of God is actually full of
demons (verse 2). Even today ungodly men hold

leadership positions in the influential denominations and religions. These false shepherds lead their sheep straight over spiritual precipices. What a monster this world force is!

Verses 8, 10, 17, 18 show that the economic collapse of the Babylonian Whore will take place in "one day"—even within "one hour" of that day. Many people could wake up to the news that a $100 bill isn't worth the ink on its face. There will be worldwide work stoppages with buyers finding no products and workers finding no employers. Further awful details appear in the rest of this chapter. With the obliteration of Satan's last human facade, the crescendoing conflict between Satan and God brings earth to Armageddon!

ARMAGEDDON

Kingdoms in Conflict

The brilliant diplomat who brought peace to a clamorous world after the Rapture of the Church has brazenly exposed his true goal: subjugation of the world and in particular the land of God's ancient people. It is the battlefield where God's heavenly hosts will wipe out the last resistance to his Son's universal kingdom of peace and justice. We need to know the identity of the mighty armies who will be involved.

The King of the South. Daniel 11 and Ezekiel 38 identify this power as Egypt. Her allies will include some of the Arab nations. Their alignment with Communist Russia already indicates some of the members of this alliance. In numbers and ferocity, it will be a formidable force.

The King of the North. Ezekiel 38 names the northern force: "Gog, of the land of Magog." This is the ancient name for Russia and the nations allied with her. They will likely include her Communist satellites in Eastern Europe, East Germany, and the Cossacks of southern Russia. Their ancient names are "Ashkenaz," "Gomer," and "Togarmah." Ethiopia and Iran seem to be pawns to be moved at Russia's will.

The Kings of the East. These are the armies from "the rising of the sun" (as some translate "East"). Asia contains the greatest numbers of potential soldiers of all areas on earth. Revelation 16:12 does not identify the Eastern armies by country, but their size seems to suggest China or/and India.

The Ten-Nation Federation. Daniel 7 and Revelation 13, 17 say to me that this is the Common Market that has now been formed in Europe. The Antichrist will eventually rule it, and, under Satan's control, the revived Roman Empire will scourge the world.

Although Megiddo in northern Israel is reasonably associated with "Armageddon," the *polemos* of Revelation 16:14 signifies an extended war or campaign; the Greek *mache* signifies battle or single combat, according to scholars Trench, Thayer, and Vincent.

As for the geographic location of the battle, I want to quote from A. Sims book, *The Coming War and the Rise of Russia* (Toronto, 1932). "It appears from Scripture that this last great battle of that great day of God Almighty will reach far beyond Armageddon, or the Valley of Megiddo. Armageddon appears to be mainly the place where the troops will gather together from the four corners of the earth, and from Armageddon the battle will spread out over the entire land of Palestine. Joel speaks of the last battle being fought in the Valley of Jehoshaphat, which is close by Jerusalem, and Isaiah shows Christ coming with blood-stained garments from 'Edom,' and Edom is south of Palestine. So the battle of Armageddon, it seems, will stretch from the Valley of Megiddo in the north of Palestine, through the Valley of Jehoshaphat, near Jerusalem, and on down to Edom at the extreme southern part of Palestine. And to this agree the words of the Prophet Ezekiel that the armies of this great battle will 'cover the land.' The Book of Revelation also says the blood will flow to the bits of the horses' bridles for 1,600 furlongs (200 miles), and it has been pointed out that 200 miles covers the entire length of Palestine. But Jerusalem will no doubt be the center of attention during the battle of Armageddon. For God's Word says: 'I will gather all nations against Jerusalem to battle.' "

Russia Pulls the Trigger

Ezekiel 38 is one of the most fascinating chapters in all of Scripture to me. It describes the beginning of the end for Russia and other nations whose governments have defied God and despised his laws. No one can exactly interpret the predicted events and their sequence, but the following account seems probable to me. Gog and Magog, motivated by hatred and greed, will reach for the mineral riches and strategic dominance of Israel and meet a hurricane of God's wrath. Verses 5, 6 list the additional nations involved in the invasion.

Persia (Iran today). Check the map and note Iran's location between Russia and Israel. I think Iran will not join the Arab federation, but instead become allied with Russia. Little Turkey and Syria cannot say much when her powerful neighbors request passage through their lands.

Ethiopia. This African nation apparently will rise to international prominence. She may become heavily in debt to Russia for armaments, and when Russia says, "Attack Israel," she has no choice—and the prospects of sure victory and much loot are great incentives.

Libya. This northern Africa nation may be joined by Algeria and other nations who are obligated to Communist "generosity." They exchanged their souls for farm machinery, tools, technicians, guns, and books.

Ezekiel 38:5 states that the above forces have been supplied with weapons. That condition has already been at least partially fulfilled by Russia.

Verse 7 says: "And you be a guide for them"; Russia is going to advise and provide leadership as well as troops.

Forward March—to Death

Satan and his demon forces have concentrated desperate efforts on earth, and his hatred of Israel, the Chosen People of God, is implacable. As a spirit being, he uses men to carry out his diabolical plans. Those he influences will share his rage against Israel. But this works into God's plan for Israel's spiritual restoration!

"In that day when my people Israel are dwelling in security, you will bestir yourself and come from your place out of the Far North, you and the many peoples with you, all of them riding on horses, a great host and a mighty army. And you will come against my people Israel like a cloud covering the land. It shall be in the latter days that I will bring you against my land, so that the nations may recognize me, when through you, Gog, I vindicate my holiness before their eyes" (Ezekiel 38:14-16).

Onward comes this great force to take the riches of Israel. "Thus says the Lord God: 'It shall be in that day that ideas shall come to mind, and you shall concoct an evil device. You will say, "I will march against the land of villages, and I will fall upon the quiet people who dwell securely without walls to defend them, without bars or gates, and I will seize booty and carry it away as plunder, assailing the waste places now inhabited and the people who were gathered from the nations, who have become possessed of cattle and goods and who dwell at the center of the earth" ' " (Ezekiel 38:10-12).

God lets them get into the mountains of Israel. Imagine the panic of the Israelis. The statement General Dayan of Israel made in 1968 may be recalled: "Our next war will not be with the Arabs; but with Russia." The brave but small Israeli army deploys for their suicide mission.

Suddenly a cliff starts to slip and with a tremendous roar it cascades down the mountain, carrying with it men and horses. Confusion erupts and Arabs fire on Africans and Russian commanders scream for order. Some try to turn back as landslides rocket down on them. Ammunition explodes and panic sets in.

Now it starts to rain. Not just a downpour, but a deluge! A virtual flood develops. Men and horses drown and plunge over cliffs. The water loosens more earth and thousands go screaming down the slopes. The rain turns to hail—gigantic ice stones, and escape is impossible. Finally, fire and brimstone lance down—perhaps from a volcano. What devastation! It's time to pay overdue accounts to God—and the debtors are going bankrupt.

"The mountains shall be thrown down; cliffs shall fall, and walls shall tumble to the ground. I will then summon the sword against him on all my mountains, says the Lord God; every man's sword shall be against his brother. With pestilence and blood I will enter into judgment with him, and I will pour upon him, upon his hordes, and upon all the nations in his train, floods of rain accompanied by hailstones, fire and brimstone" (Ezekiel 38:20-22).

"I stand against you, Gog, leader of Meshech and Tubal. I will turn you and drive you toward the mountains of Israel, bringing you from the distant North. And I will destroy 85 percent of your army in the mountains. I will knock your weapons from your hands and leave you helpless. You and all your vast armies will die upon the mountains. I will give you to the wild animals and vultures to devour you. You will never reach the cities—you will fall upon the open fields; for I have spoken, the Lord God says" (Ezekiel 39:1-5).

Ezekiel describes Israel taking seven months to bury the dead and seven years to gather the weapons and spoil. But most important of all is the fact that many in Israel see this act of deliverance for what it really is: a divine act of mercy and deliverance, and one-third of them will turn to God and accept his Christ as their Messiah (cf. Zechariah 13:8, 9; Ezekiel 39:25-29).

Meanwhile, Back with the Beast

As soon as the Antichrist learns of Russia's designs on Israel, he moves his crack armies into the Holy Land to "protect" her. Using as an excuse the treaty he made—and broke by desecrating the temple—he occupies the land without invitation. When the news gets out about extraordinary forces decimating Russia's armies, various reactions are seen.

The devil convinces the Antichrist he destroyed Russia so the Beast can plunder Israel.

Iran, Libya, Algiers, East Germany, and the satellite countries crawl back to any hole they can find.

Egypt is furious at being double-crossed. She has pledged to push the Jews into the sea and now recognizes the Beast isn't about to give up Jerusalem.

A Ghastly Replay

Egypt quickly mobilizes her forces for attack. She contacts the Russian government and finds officials angry at their troops' performance, not fearful about what happened in the mountains of Israel. She mobilizes her remaining forces and prepares to invade.

It doesn't take long to align nations against the Beast. They decide to attack Jerusalem by land and sea—Daniel was very clear about the navy participating in this attack (chapter 11). Russia's ships have dominated the Mediterranean for some time.

The results of this invasion and defense are found in Zechariah 12, 13, and 14. The city of Jerusalem is almost flattened by the blast of the attack. "On that day the Lord will gather together the nations to fight Jerusalem; the city will be taken, the houses rifled, the loot divided, the women raped; half the population will be taken away as slaves, and half will be left in what remains of the city" (Zechariah 14:1).

But the armies of the Beast are victorious over Russia and Egypt (Daniel 11:40). His military machine rolls until he orders a halt. "He will invade various lands on the way, including Israel, the Pleasant Land, and overthrow the governments of many nations. . . . He will capture all the treasures of Egypt, and the Libyans and Ethiopians shall be his servants" (Daniel 11:41-43).

Some Bible commentators interpret the King of the North as being Russia instead of the Antichrist. I believe Daniel 11:40 refers to the Antichrist for the following reasons:

Ezekiel 39:1-5 clearly states that Russia will come from the North to the *mountains* of Israel where 85 percent of their armies will be destroyed. God will even rain down fire on those at home— "dwelling securely by the coast" (39:6).

In Russia's panic fight, they'll keep dying in fields (39:5) so that men will be assigned the responsibility of searching for the bodies to bury them (39:14).

Gog and Magog (Russia) are identified repeatedly in prophecy but not mentioned in Daniel 11.

A note in *The Living Bible,* referring to Daniel 11:40, says: "The prophecy takes a turn here . . . the Antichrist of the last days becomes the center of attention from this point on."

In Zechariah we have the best picture of what will happen to Russia and Egypt. " 'In that day,' says the Lord, 'I will bewilder the armies drawn up against her, and make fools of them; for I will watch over the people of Judah, but blind her enemies' " (12:4). "And the Lord will send a plague on all the people who fought Jerusalem. They will become

like walking corpses, their flesh rotting away; their
eyes will shrivel in their sockets, and the tongues
will decay in their mouths. They will be seized
with terror, panic-stricken from the Lord, and will
fight each other in hand-to-hand combat" (14:12,
13).

What else but a nuclear fire storm could cause
"flesh to rot," and "eyes to shrivel in their sockets"
and "tongues to decay in their mouths"—while on
their feet? The incalculable heat and force of multi-
ple-megaton explosions cremate people before they
can fall.

So the Beast and his armies occupy Egypt and
capture her treasure. The prophecy of Isaiah is fulfilled: "And I will give the Egyptians into the hand
of a cruel master; a fierce king will reign over them,
says the Lord of hosts" (Isaiah 19:4).

Eventually Egypt's pride and foolish trust in
astrology and false gods ends, Isaiah says. "So she
will cry to the Lord because of their oppressors;
and the Lord will send a Savior, even a mighty one,
and he will deliver them" (19:20).

God hears and answers Egypt! Who can know
the love of God? For centuries these people have
followed false prophets and persecuted the descendants of Abraham, but mercy is still available to
them. God even says, "Blessed be Egypt, my people" (Isaiah 19:25). How great thou art!

Challenge from the East

While the Beast and his armies are penetrating
Egypt and Africa, news arrives that causes him to

return hurriedly to Israel. The mighty battalions from the East—200 million strong—have begun massing on the banks of the Euphrates River. The message is clear. With such a formidable force and possibly nuclear weapons, the Kings of the East have decided to challenge the authority of the Beast. "But then news from the east and north will alarm him and he will return in great anger to destroy as he goes" (Daniel 11:44).

For some reason the mighty army stops at the Euphrates River, but not for long. The river suddenly runs dry. "The sixth angel poured out his flask upon the great River Euphrates and it dried up so that the Kings from the East could march their armies westward without hindrance" (Revelation 16:12).

Kill! Kill! Kill!

Earth will seem like hell when the four mighty demons who have been bound in the Euphrates River are released. They resemble psychopathic killers and are able to instill their murderous personality in Christ-rejecting men. Normal restraints are removed and the evil forces of hell energize mankind. ". . . the four mighty demons held bound at the great River Euphrates . . . had been kept in readiness for that year and month and day and hour, and now they were turned loose to kill a third of all mankind. They led an army of 200 million warriors—I heard an announcement of how many there were" (Revelation 9:14-16).

Did you notice verse 15—the *year, month, day,* and even *hour?* Man, if you ever doubted God's timing or control, if you ever wondered whether he has a plan and knows what's happening—be convinced. I'm glad I know him! He's got a year, month, day, and hour schedule for me, too. He's also got one for you he'll gladly work out if you'll let him.

Ask a veteran of World War II what a *banzai* attack by the Japanese was. He'll tell you it was a human wave of Japanese soldiers whose passion to kill made them ferocious opponents. China has indicated her endorsement of "human waves." Korean veterans saw it used, and Red China was directing that war. The added viciousness of demon compulsion makes the horror beyond imagination.

But there is more. Revelation 9:17-19 seems to suggest nuclear weapons. Fire! Smoke and flaming sulphur! Death by the millions!

Diabolical Double-Cross

Satan, the master deceiver, has a diabolical double-cross going! He is playing both sides against the middle. Those are his demons that turned the Eastern armies into kill-crazed fiends, and all the time he's impelling the Antichrist against that dreadnought. His real target is Israel and its destruction.

The effects of this havoc on survivors are incredible! "The men left alive after these plagues still refused to worship God! They would not renounce their demon-worship, nor their idols made of gold and silver, brass, stone, and wood—which neither see nor hear nor walk. Neither did they change their mind and attitude about all their murders and witchcraft, their immorality and theft" (Revelation 9:20, 21).

Evidently these spiritually blind men can see no glimmer of light from God.

Leap Frog

"And I saw three evil spirits disguised as frogs leap from the mouth of the Dragon [Satan], the Creature [Beast], and his False Prophet. These miracle-working demons conferred with all the rulers of the world to gather them for battle against the Lord on that great coming judgment day of God Almighty. And they gathered all the armies of the world near a place called, in Hebrew, Armageddon" (Revelation 16:13, 14, 16).

Notice the words "against the Lord." These nations are indeed gathered to fight against the Lord, but they do not realize it. Evil spirits have convinced them to march against Israel to gain peace for the world. And so they gathered in the place God said they would—for the last stand of Satan and his followers against Christ.

Look Up—and Die

Many men may die of fright as the Lord shakes the universe before appearing on earth. Matthew 24:29 gives Jesus' prophecies of four cosmic events: the sun darkens; the moon turns black; stars start falling; and the powers overshadowing the earth—gravity, magnetic forces, and orbit patterns—are convulsed. No one will miss these signals!

But the sequel is the stunner. According to the Apostle John's vision, the skies unveil a white horse with a majestic figure seated on him. The rider's eyes are like flames of fire and his crowns confirm his royalty; his title is written clearly for all to see: "King of kings and Lord of lords" (cf. Revelation 19:11-16).

The celestial army is equally impressive. The prophet Joel gives a beautiful description. "What a mighty army! It covers the mountains like night! How great, how powerful these people are! The likes of them have not been seen before, and never will again throughout the generations of the world! Fire goes before them and follows them on every side! Ahead of them the land lies fair as Eden's Garden in all its beauty, but they destroy it to the ground; not one thing escapes. They look like tiny horses, and they run as fast. Look at them leaping along the tops of the mountains! Listen to the noise they make, like the rumbling of chariots, or the roar of fire sweeping across a field, and like a mighty army moving into battle.

"Fear grips the waiting people; their faces grow pale with fright. These soldiers charge like infantry; they scale the walls like picked and trained commandos. Straight forward they march, never breaking ranks. They never crowd each other. Each is right in place; no weapon can stop them. They swarm upon the city; they run upon the walls; they climb up into the windows. The earth quakes before them and the heavens tremble. The sun and moon are obscured and the stars are hid. The Lord leads them with a shout. This is his mighty army and they follow his orders. The day of the judgment of the Lord is an awesome, terrible thing. Who can endure it? That is why the Lord says: Turn to me now, while there is time. Give me all your hearts" (Joel 2:2-12).

Satan will be desperate. He tries to reprogram the armies of the nations to fight this new enemy descending from the sky. But it's hopeless for the Beast, Satan's prime minister on earth. Daniel predicted as much long ago. "He will halt between Jerusalem and the sea, and there pitch his royal tents, but while he is there his time will suddenly run out and there will be no one to help him" (11:45).

The Mountain Splits

"That day his feet will stand upon the Mount of Olives, to the east of Jerusalem; and the Mount of Olives will split apart, making a very wide valley running from east to west; for half the mountain will move toward the north and half toward the south" (Zechariah 14:4).

A large oil company doing surveys of the area around Jerusalem discovered a tremendous fault running through the center of the Mount of Olives —a rock division running east and west. It is said a motel chain rejected this property for this underground weakness.

There is a group of believers in Jerusalem whom God is going to spare—but how? The Beast is camped between Jerusalem and the sea, and the

armies of the East are charging from the other
direction toward the northern plains where God
said all nations will be gathered. As the Lord parted
the sea for his people in the past, he will now open
a *mountain* and they will rush through the valley
to safety.

"You will escape through the valley, for it will
reach across to the city gate. Yes, you will escape
as your people did long centuries ago from the
earthquake in the days of Uzziah, king of Judah;
and the Lord my God shall come, and all his saints
and angels with him" (Zechariah 14:5).

Notice who will be with Jesus in this action: "all
his saints"—that's me, and *you* if you're his child
by faith.

The Lake of Fire

There are not many details given about the fate
of the Beast and the False Prophet—but they are
fearful and unmistakable. Revelation 19:20 tells
it all: "And the Evil Creature was captured, and
with him the False Prophet . . . both of them were
thrown alive into the lake of fire that burns with
sulphur."

Satan is not with them, but he has not escaped.
His fate for the time being is different. "Then I saw
an angel come down from heaven with the key to
the bottomless pit and a heavy chain in his hand.
He seized the Dragon—that old Serpent, the devil,
Satan—and bound him in chains for 1,000 years,
and threw him into the bottomless pit, which he
then shut and locked, so that he could not fool the

nations any more until the thousand years were finished. Afterwards he would be released again for a little while" (Revelation 20:1-3).

The vanquished armies end ignominiously. Vulturous birds are summoned to "come and feast on the flesh of kings, and captains, and great generals; of horses and riders; and of all humanity; both great and small. . . . And their entire army was killed with the sharp sword in the mouth of the one riding the white horse, and all the birds of heaven were gorged with their flesh" (Revelation 19:18, 21).

Then all the remaining people on earth will be marshalled before the throne of Christ to be judged. Their judgment will be based on their treatment of "Jesus' brethren," the Jews. No one enters the Kingdom of God without a personal relationship with Christ, but during the Tribulation the evidence of faith is willingness to help the persecuted and suffering Jews. Jesus clearly forecast his assessment: "For I was hungry and you fed me; I was thirsty and you gave me water; I was a stranger and you invited me into your homes; naked and you clothed me; sick and in prison, and you visited me." "When did we ever see you hungry and feed you? . . ." "And I, the King, will tell them, 'When you did it to these my brothers you were doing it to me!' " (Matthew 25:35, 37, 40).

The same chapter describes the fate of unbelievers. For the reasons given above, those who showed no faith will hear these words: "Away with you, cursed ones, into the eternal fire prepared for the devil and his demons" (25:41).

So now the world is purged of all unbelievers. Humanity is given a new start, under a perfect King.

The Super Supper

All the saints—that's "believers"—of the Old Testament and the Tribulation will be invited to this marriage feast. The Christians of the New Testament era are the honored guests of Jesus, the Bridegroom.

There Jesus Christ will present us, his bride, to the rest of the saints. John the Baptist will be there. ("I am the Bridegroom's friend, and I am filled with joy at his success"—John 3:29.) So will Abraham, Isaac, and Jacob. Moses and Elijah and other patriarchs will give us honor as the bride of the Son of God.

Remember, the marriage took place in heaven after the Rapture of the Church, but now the banquet takes place on earth. "Let us be glad and rejoice and honor him; for the time has come for the wedding banquet of the Lamb, and his bride has prepared herself. She is permitted to wear the cleanest and whitest and finest of linens. And the angel dictated this sentence to me: blessed are those who are invited to the wedding feast of the Lamb. And he added: God himself has stated this" (Revelation 19:7-9).

I'm sure the parable of Matthew 25 about the wise and foolish virgins applies to this event. William L. Pettingill points out that Matthew 25:1 reads like this in the Latin Vulgate: "Then shall the kingdom of heaven be likened unto ten virgins, who took their lamps, and went forth to meet the Bridegroom and bride."

Verse 10 in *The Living Bible* reads, "But while they were gone, the Bridegroom came, and those who were ready went in with him to the marriage feast, and the door was locked."

Inside, the celebration begins.

7

PEACE AT LAST

It's called the Millennium. That means 1,000 years—and in this case it means many other wonderful things for the people of God's kingdom. There is more prophetic Scripture written on the Millennium than any other subject. It's going to be a fantastic time of joy, though for some it will also be a time of testing. During the Millennium God will prove some thrilling promises made to his chosen people, the Jews.

First, to Abraham. God chose Abraham as the father of a people whom he would prosper and flood with favors.

"So I will not destroy all Israel, for I have true servants there. I will preserve a remnant of my people to possess the land of Israel; those I select will inherit it and serve me there" (Isaiah 65:8, 9).

"But I will bring my people back again from all the countries where in my fury I will scatter them. I will bring them back to this very city, and make them live in peace and safety. And they shall be my people and I will be their God. And I will make an everlasting covenant with them, promising never again to desert them, but only to do them good. I will put a desire into their hearts to worship me, and they shall never leave me. I will rejoice to do them good and will replant them in this land, with great joy. Just as I have sent all these terrors and evils upon them, so will I do all the good I have promised them" (Jeremiah 32:36-38, 40-42).

Second, to David. Israel's greatest king was promised a perpetual Successor.

"For the time is coming, says the Lord, when I will place a righteous Branch upon King David's throne. He shall be a King who shall rule with wisdom and justice and cause righteousness to prevail everywhere throughout the earth. And this is his name: The Lord Our Righteousness. At that time Judah will be saved and Israel will live in peace" (Jeremiah 23:5, 6).

"'In that day he who created the royal dynasty of David will be a banner of salvation to all the world. The nations will rally to him, for the land where he lives will be a glorious place" (Isaiah 11:10).

Third, concerning Canaan, the land promised

permanently to Abraham's descendants.

"And you shall live in Israel, the land that I gave your fathers long ago. And you shall be my people and I shall be your God. I will cleanse away your sins. I will abolish crop failures and famine. I will give you huge harvests from your fruit trees and fields" (Ezekiel 36:28-30).

"Then the people of Judah and Israel will unite and have one leader; they will return from exile together; what a day that will be—the day when God will sow his people in the fertile soil of their own land again" (Hosea 1:11).

"The time will come, O Israel, when I will gather you — all that are left — and bring you together again. . . . The Messiah will lead you out of exile and bring you through the gates of your cities of captivity, back to your own land. Your King will go before you—the Lord leads on" (Micah 2:12, 13).

Fourth, concerning a new heart.

"And when you return you will remove every trace of all this idol worship. I will give you one heart and a new spirit; I will take from you your hearts of stone and give you tender hearts of love for God" (Ezekiel 11:18, 19).

"The day will come, says the Lord, when I will make a new contract with the people of Israel and Judah. It won't be like the one I made with their fathers . . . a contract they broke, forcing me to reject them, says the Lord. But this is the new contract I will make with them: I will inscribe my laws upon their hearts, so that they shall want to honor me; then they shall truly be my people and I will be their God" (Jeremiah 31:31-33).

The Kingdom Come

Christ's great kingdom shall come to earth and "the government will be upon his shoulders." The form of government will be theocratic—a government with God as ruler. No more necessity for separating of church and state. No more political games to push the Prince of Peace out of the way so men can work out a peace plan.

This government will praise and reward righteousness, so men will think positively and kindly. The ruler of this government will be available and lovingly interested in all people. Here are a few characteristics of his kingdom on earth.

Obedience. After the universal corruption created by mankind, the breaking of every major contract and the violation of every law, this period will be a delight to God as well as man. Satan is bound, so there is no temptation. Every person will understand God's will.

Truth. In Romans 1, we can see man's style, and we know it well because we live under it now. But the one who said he is the Truth is reigning in the Millennium. "He will judge all nations fairly" (Psalm 96:10).

Holiness. We who now possess the Holy Spirit get so fouled up with this world's materialism and rationalism that we grieve him, quench him, and restrict his supernatural power to a few manifestations. In the Millennium everyone will be aware of

Christ's love and mercy as well as his power and purity.

Imagine a society where neighbors follow the Golden Rule and family members actually love each other!

How Sweet It Is

A new age has begun. The age of grace brings people to eternal life through faith. The Tribulation brings wrath and judgment to irreconcilable men. The Millennium brings overflowing blessings to humanity on earth, who—remember—have physical bodies and a human civilization as at present because they are survivors of the Tribulation conflagration.

"In that day the wolf and the lamb will lie down together, and the leopard and goats will be at peace. Calves and fat cattle will be safe among lions, and a little child shall lead them all. The cows will graze among bears; cubs and calves will lie down together, and lions will eat grass like the cows. Babies will crawl safely among poisonous snakes, and a little child who puts his hand in a nest of deadly adders will pull it out unharmed. Nothing will hurt or destroy in all my holy mountain. For as the waters fill the sea, so shall the earth be full of the knowledge of the Lord" (Isaiah 11:6-9).

What a time that will be!

Peace—no more war. "The Lord will settle international disputes; all the nations will convert their weapons of war into implements of peace. Then at last all wars will stop and all military training will end" (Isaiah 2:4).

Joy—young and old will take part in the fun. "The young girls will dance for joy, and men folk—old and young—will take their part in all the fun; for I will turn their mourning into joy and I will comfort them and make them rejoice, for their captivity with all its sorrows will be behind them" (Jeremiah 31:13).

Healing—deaf will hear; blind see. "In that day the deaf will hear the words of a book, and out of their gloom and darkness the blind will see my plans" (Isaiah 29:18).

Health—given by God. "I will give you back your health again and heal your wounds. Now you are called 'The Outcast' and 'Jerusalem, the Place Nobody Wants' " (Jeremiah 30:17).

Prosperity—even deserts will be green. "Even the wilderness and desert will rejoice in those days; the desert will blossom with flowers. Yes, there will be an abundance of flowers and singing and joy! The deserts will become as green as the Lebanon mountains, as lovely as Mount Carmel's pastures and Sharon's meadows; for the Lord will display his glory there, the excellency of our God" (Isaiah 35:1, 2).

One language. "At that time I will change the speech of my returning people to pure Hebrew so that all can worship the Lord together" (Zephaniah 3:9).

Freedom. "In that wonderful day when the Lord gives his people rest from sorrow and fear, from slavery and chains. . . . But at last the whole earth

is at rest and is quiet! All the world begins to sing!"
(Isaiah 14:3, 7).

Full knowledge. "And the Spirit of the Lord
shall rest upon him, the Spirit of wisdom, under-
standing, counsel and might; the Spirit of knowledge
and of the fear of the Lord" (Isaiah 11:2).

Families and birth. "When I whistle to them,
they'll come running, for I have bought them back
again. From the few that are left, their population
will grow again to former size" (Zechariah 10:8).

These are just a few of the conditions of the
Millennium. Isaiah 65:16-25 also gives a beautiful
picture of this time. Here are a few verses from
the passage. "For I will put aside my anger and
forget the evil that you did. For see, I am creating
new heavens and a new earth—so wonderful that
no one will even think about the old ones any more.
Be glad; rejoice forever in my creation. . . . No
longer will babies die when only a few days old;
no longer will men be considered old at 100! Only
sinners will die that young. . . . I will answer them
before they even call to me. While they are still
talking to me about their needs, I will go ahead
and answer their prayer."

Perhaps you paused at the phrase: "Only sinners
will die that young," and wondered what it meant.
It means that in spite of the perfect government of
truth and justice, in spite of the presence and power
of Jesus Christ, in spite of the fabulous conditions
of the Millennium, in spite of the personal rule of
the Lord himself, humans will still act like humans.
They will have every opportunity by environment

and example to live holy lives, and yet some will rebel and sin. They will still be born with natural ego and selfishness, also the ability to choose their life-style. Obviously, the wrong choice results in early death.

Some nations will become lax in their worship and will be punished for it. "In the end, those who survive the plague will go up to Jerusalem each year to worship the King, the Lord of Hosts, to celebrate a time of thanksgiving. And any nation anywhere in all the world that refuses to come to Jerusalem to worship the King, the Lord of Hosts, will have no rain" (Zechariah 14:16, 17).

Don't be surprised by this. In Revelation 19:15 the authoritative rule of Christ during the Millennium, as far as the rebellious are concerned, is made clear: "and he shall rule them with a rod of iron."

So the Millennium will be a time of testing—and failure—for some. Men born during the Golden Age, under ideal conditions, are sinful by nature and their pride must be willingly subordinated to Christ.

We Will Rule

Believers who have been raptured, made fully righteous, and married to Christ, will not again be subjected to temptation and trial. Rather we will rule with Christ, having taken part in the first resurrection. "Blessed and holy are those who share in the first resurrection. For them the second death holds no terrors, for they will be priests of God and of Christ, and shall reign with him a thousand years" (Revelation 20:6). "And you have gathered them into a kingdom and made them priests of our God; they shall reign upon the earth" (Revelation 5:10).

Christ is King during the Millennium, and we are his royal priesthood: "For you have been chosen by God himself—you are priests of the King, you are holy and pure, you are God's very own" (1 Peter 2:9).

Look Out! Satan's Loose

One of the most astounding prophecies of all appears in Revelation 20:7-9. "When the thousand years end, Satan will be let out of his prison. He will go out to deceive the nations of the world and gather them together, with Gog and Magog, for battle—a mighty host, numberless as sand along the shore. They will go up across the broad plain of the earth and surround God's people and the beloved city of Jerusalem on every side."

Can man be so stupid and depraved as to live in a perfect society and still not be content? The awful answer is "Yes!"

The lies and empty promises of Satan will obviously be believed by many because the number is so great it can't be counted.

Perhaps you ask, "Why would God allow Satan to tempt and deceive people again?" For the same reason the Tree of Life was placed in the Garden of Eden. To give man a choice! God wants men to trust him, love him, and obey him because they *want* to—not because they are forced to. So the time of choice or testing has come and those who stand faithful will dwell with the Lord eternally. But those who fall will be lost forever.

"But fire from God in heaven will flash down on the attacking armies and consume them. Then the devil who had betrayed them again will be thrown into the lake of fire burning with sulphur where the Creature and False Prophet are, and they will be tormented day and night forever and ever" (Revelation 20:9, 10)

Satan—and evil—are finished for good.

The Great White Throne

There is a group of people who have not yet received their "wages of sin."

These are individuals who died in their sins and they await their judgment.

"And I saw a Great White Throne and the one who sat upon it, from whose face the earth and sky fled away, but they found no place to hide. I saw the dead, great and small, standing before God; and the Books were opened including the Book of Life. And the dead were judged according to the things written in the Books, each according to the deeds he had done. The oceans surrendered up the bodies buried in them; and the earth and the underworld gave up the dead in them. Each was judged according to his deeds. And death and hell were thrown into the Lake of Fire. This is the second death—the Lake of Fire (Revelation 20:11-14).

This is an awesome account of the thoroughness with which God keeps records. He knows us so well he has a record of every deed ever done. Notice the reference to "Books." The judgment of each of these condemned persons will be based on what's written in those Books.

This is the "second resurrection." There are no believers here; only the unsaved dead of all times (cf. John 5:29). "Blessed and holy are those who share in the first resurrection. For them the second death holds no terrors" (Revelation 20:6).

People at the Great White Throne have chosen their path and destiny. Jesus made a way to heaven, and these persons "loved the darkness more than the light" (John 3:19).

Why then are the Books of man's deeds needed or used? I believe for two reasons. First, to substantiate the justice of the sentence. The account of each man's rejections is recorded: every time he scoffed at righteousness, every time he squelched a conviction in his soul, every time he relished evil. There will be no doubt on anyone's part as to the fairness of the decision.

Second, the works must be recorded to determine the degree of punishment. *All* unbelievers will be punished, and their punishment will be terrible. "And if anyone's name was not found recorded in the Book of Life, he was thrown into the Lake of Fire" (Revelation 20:15). But Luke 12:47, 48 teaches a difference in the intensity of punishment based on knowledge and works. "He will be severely punished, for though he knew his duty he refused to do it. But anyone who is not aware that he is doing wrong will be punished only lightly.

Much is required from those to whom much is given, for their responsibility is greater."

In Matthew 11 Jesus denounces the cities where he had performed most of his miracles, because they hadn't turned to God. Listen to what he says to Capernaum, and remember the "cities" he is talking to are made up of people, not walls and houses. "And Capernaum, though highly honored, shall go down to hell. For if the marvelous miracles I did in you had been done in Sodom, it would still be here today. Truly, Sodom will be better off at the judgment day than you" (11:23, 24).

The Book

Along with the mention of "Books," in Revelation 20 we have the "Book." This is the Book of Life. God keeps very complete records. In this case, if your name is recorded in the Book of Life you are his child and will forever dwell with him. At the moment of your spiritual birth—when you receive Jesus Christ by faith—your name is written down and the record of your old life and deeds (in the "Books") is destroyed. In both Jeremiah and Hebrews, the Bible speaks of God forgetting these sins.

If you have not experienced this miracle and want to, just admit to God that you're a sinner—though you may be a church member or can name at least five people who are worse than you—and tell him you believe Jesus, his Son, died for you; ask him to forgive you, and tell him you are receiving Christ as your personal Savior by faith. Do it now. Pray the above sentence as your own prayer, and God will hear and receive you.

Before you finish this encounter with God, he writes your name in the Book of Life and removes your sins from his memory. You are a royal child. Now act like it! Read the Bible; it will be more meaningful now that you know the Author. Find a church that preaches Christ as Savior and the Bible as the true Word of God.

Welcome to the family. I'll see you in heaven, and reign with you on earth! Here are a couple of our Father's promises; claim them now.

"Come to me with your ears wide open. Listen, for the life of your soul is at stake. I am ready to make an everlasting covenant with you, to give you unfailing mercies and love" (Isaiah 55:3).

"Seek the Lord while you can find him. Call upon him now while he is near. Let men cast off their wicked deeds; let them banish from their minds the very thought of doing wrong! Let them turn to the Lord that he may have mercy upon them, and to our God, for he will abundantly pardon!" (Isaiah 55:6, 7).

The World's on Fire

"Then I saw a new earth, with no oceans, and a new sky, for the present earth and sky had disappeared" (Revelation 21:1). That isn't much detail as to what happened, but Peter was given a little more information. "And God has commanded that the earth and the heavens be stored away for a great bonfire at the judgment day, when all ungodly men will perish. . . . And then the heavens will pass away with a terrible noise and the heavenly bodies will disappear in fire, and the earth and everything on it will be burned up. And so everything around us is going to melt away. . . Look forward to that day and hurry it along—the day when God will set the heavens on fire, and the heavenly bodies will melt and disappear in flames" (2 Peter 3:7, 10, 12, 13).

Fire will be the means of judging the world in the last days. Water was used the first time and only the earth was involved; the heavens, both atmosphere and space, will be included in this judgment.

We know we're dwelling on a ball of molten heat. Every now and then a little piece blows off and we get the fearful picture of what's under us. We call it volcanic eruption and lava. I read that the word "element" as used in 2 Peter 3 means a basic article of nature. Nothing is more basic than the atom. Everything, however immense, begins with one. The same translator gives the literal meaning of "destroy" as "to loose" or "let go." God is probably going to "undo" the atoms. You know what happens when one is split. Then they'll all come apart in a raging fire storm. How can man's mind imagine the roar of a worldwide volcano or the blast of billions of megatons of nuclear energy. All Peter could say was, "The heavens will pass away with a terrible noise and the heavenly bodies will disappear in fire, and the earth and everything on it will be burned up." The reason is seen in the

holiness of God described in Hebrews 12:29—"For
our God is a consuming fire!"

The Lord's City

Oceans have separated countries and men; they
have been treacherous and stormy, bringing fear
and death. The constructive contributions—evapo-
ration, dissolution, and food supply will not be
needed in the New Earth. Peter assures us: "But
we are looking forward to God's promise of new
heavens and a new earth afterwards, where there
will be only goodness" (2 Peter 3:13).

Now that the earth and heavens have been made
ready, the "New Jerusalem" or "Holy City" will
descend from above. It will be beyond imagining.
Remember that Jesus said: "There are many homes
up there where my Father lives, and I am going to
prepare them for your coming" (John 14:1, 2).

Old Testament saints also had a hope for a better
place. "Abraham . . . was confidently waiting for
God to bring him to that strong heavenly city whose
designer and builder is God" (Hebrews 11:10). "He
has made a heavenly city for them" (11:16).

John describes this city in detail in Revelation
21. He saw it descending out of the skies; he says
it was filled with the glory of God and flashed and
glowed.

It will be 1,500 miles each way. The walls will be
216 feet thick and the whole city will be trans-
parent, gold-like glass. The foundations, all twelve
layers, are inlaid with twelve different gems—emer-
alds, sapphires, topazes, amethysts, and others.

There will be twelve gates, each made from a single pearl. And the main street will be pure gold.

The light from the Holy City hovering over the earth will light the globe. There will be no moon or sun; God and Christ will illuminate all. Night will no longer exist. And those who are going to reside there are "those whose names are written in the Lamb's Book of Life" (Revelation 21:27).

"And he pointed out to me a river of pure water of life, clear as crystal, flowing from the Throne of God and the Lamb, coursing down the center of the main street. On each side of the river grew trees of life. . . . There shall be nothing in the city which is evil; for the Throne of God and of the Lamb will be there, and his servants will worship him.

"And they shall see his face; and his name shall be written on their foreheads. And there will be no night there—no need for lamps or sun—for the Lord God will be their light; and they shall reign forever and ever" (22:1-5).

Majesty! Glory! Power!

The words are trustworthy and true:
"I AM COMING SOON!"
God told his prophets what the future holds— blessed are those who believe it!
"I AM COMING SOON!"
He who has said all these things declares:
"I AM COMING SOON!"
Amen! *Come, Lord Jesus!*

(Revelation 22)